# BONDS OF DESTINY

# BONDS OF DESTINY
~ THE LEGACY ~

## RAJESH VARMA

Published by
Rupa Publications India Pvt. Ltd 2017
7/16, Ansari Road, Daryaganj
New Delhi 110002

*Sales centres:*
Allahabad Bengaluru Chennai
Hyderabad Jaipur Kathmandu
Kolkata Mumbai

Copyright © Rajesh Varma 2017

The views and opinions expressed in this book are the author's own and the facts are as reported by him which have been verified to the extent possible, and the publishers are not in any way liable for the same.

All rights reserved.
No part of this publication may be reproduced, transmitted, or stored in a retrieval system, in any form or by any means, electronic, mechanical, photocopying, recording or otherwise, without the prior permission of the publisher.

ISBN: 978-81-291-4800-1

First impression 2017

10 9 8 7 6 5 4 3 2 1

Printed at HT Media Ltd, Noida

This book is sold subject to the condition that it shall not, by way of trade or otherwise, be lent, resold, hired out, or otherwise circulated, without the publisher's prior consent, in any form of binding or cover other than that in which it is published.

*For my father.*
*Without him the narrative would not exist.*

And you, my father, there on the sad height,
Curse, bless me now with your fierce tears, I pray.
Do not go gentle into that good night.
Rage, rage against the dying of the light.

—Dylan Thomas,
*Do Not Go Gentle Into That Good Night*

## Contents

| | |
|---|---:|
| *Foreword* | xi |
| *Preface* | xv |
| An Act of Faith | 1 |
| People Will Get to Read My Story | 19 |
| A Collector of Worlds | 29 |
| End of the War, Beginning of the Battle | 69 |
| But It Was Not Meant to Be | 75 |
| The Hidden Hand of Destiny | 86 |
| The Reunion | 111 |

| | |
|---|---|
| A Bet We Both Won | 122 |
| The Letter | 131 |
| *Epilogue* | 135 |
| *Acknowledgements* | 139 |

# Foreword

Navdeep Suri
*India's Ambassador to UAE*

It was way back in 1980 that I met Rajesh Varma at the verdant, sprawling and still developing campus of Guru Nanak Dev University in Amritsar. We were doing our Masters in Economics and although I was a year senior, we quickly struck a warm friendship. Rajesh, even then, was a bit different—deeper, contemplative and sensitive about those around him. It set him apart from the rest of our carefree, boisterous bunch.

That sensitivity is manifest throughout *Bonds of Destiny*, a moving story of Shingara Singh, passed on by Bhushan to his son Rajesh. Many of us would have probably heard other such stories from our parents, only to tuck them away in some deep recesses of our memory. I can say with all honesty that I am no different. That's what I did with the tales that we heard from my grandfather Nanak Singh. Indeed, as we were growing up in Amritsar and spending our summer vacations in our village Preet Nagar, my childhood was a treasure house of tales told by the greatest story-teller of his generation—one who is now regarded as the Father of the Punjabi novel. Some of these had a strong autobiographical touch, others were woven around the realities of the times. And yet, not once did we think of digging deeper into the stories, of trying to establish a personal connection with any of the characters.

Rajesh is clearly cut from a different fabric. He inherited a profoundly poignant story from his father and then took it a step further to make himself an integral character in the evolving narrative. His first visit to Ghasitpura with Arti to connect with Shingara Singh's family, his intuitive bond with the family and his visit ten years later to introduce his children to Bahadur Singh, Jarnail and the next generation is truly extraordinary. Living a world away in distant California, it takes a very special kind of empathy to make that effort, to come all the way to an impoverished village in Punjab, to establish second and third generation connections with the family of one who had served his father some seventy years ago.

The story itself takes us into Nagaland in India's north-east, into a distant and oft-forgotten theatre of the Second World War that pitted British troops against the advancing Japanese army, throwing Indian soldiers fighting against their own brethren of the Indian National Army. Do you support Mahatma Gandhi's approach to support the British war effort and secure independence in return, or do you support Netaji Subhash Chandra Bose's more militant approach of joining the enemy of the enemy to defeat the British on the battlefield? The spirit of nationalism in Bhushan and his team, their burning desire to strive for India's independence is palpable, as is the dilemma inherent in fighting an alien war where they are supporting the oppressor.

Like any good yarn, this story retains an element of suspense till the very end. And it comes with a message. At a time when the world is obsessed with material goods, where ambition and the race to get ahead often trump human relations, this book serves as a timely reminder of the things that really matter. The 'bonds of destiny' between Bhushan's and Shingara Singh's families are not unique. What makes them special is the way they have been nurtured. I hope this book inspires us to seek out similar bonds that we may have encountered in our own lives, to establish those special relationships in a way that we enrich our own lives and those of others.

20 July 2017

# Preface

Like many children, I grew up listening to stories from my father. Some of these were true events of his life. At the time they were narrated to me, it felt as if they were disjointed episodes. The stories were whispered to me during those moments of father-son bonding when I would demand my father to snuggle with me at bedtime and tell me a story from when he was young. Each night's story picked up where the previous one left off. Our routine was predictable. I would lie down next to him, rest my head on his left shoulder, and turn to my right, while he would lie down on his back, gently patting my head with his right hand. Once comfortable, I would be ready to roll the film of vibrant images from my father's tales the night before. I would remind my father where he had ended the previous night and this would be followed by, 'Papa, then what happened?'

Our routine worked well. He knew that the alternative—reading aloud from a children's story book—was not something that I enjoyed. Fiction did not appeal to me. I knew it was not true. Besides, reading the story book meant that I could not lie next to my father, something that made me feel closer to him. Looking back, I think our arrangement made things easier for my father as well. All he had to do was to recall one of those incidents, and bring it to life through narration as though he were passing on to me precious gems he had safely stored in his memory.

He never began his stories with the usual 'Once upon a time…' Each night I would ask, 'Papa, then what happened?', and he would begin with, 'And then one day, when…' and the story would continue.

*Bonds of Destiny* is a necklace strewn with these precious gems that were passed on to me by my father. Stringing them together was no mean task. The stories that construe these gems were strewn over a vast landscape spanning almost seventy years, beginning with the early 1920s around the time when my father, Bhushan[1] was born, and decades later

---

[1] My father's given name was Dev Brat, but everyone in the family lovingly called him Bhushan. His friends and his colleagues would address him as Varma Sahib or Varmaji. I have chosen to use the name that was used by his family—Bhushan.

taking me to varied locales and eras as I tracked people and places to find the missing pieces that would finally let me put it all together.

It became obvious to me once I started stringing these gems together that numerous links—including details and the final outcome of a key incident—had not been passed on to me on those warm, comforting and special nights. As I explored further, I realized they had been left out on purpose. Not that I noticed it then.

An essential part of childhood innocence is that children simply listen and absorb. They do not question much. I was not any different. It never occurred to me to ask for details, or for the missing links connected with the key episode or incident that forms the foundation of this book.

By the time I started putting together *Bonds of Destiny* in the early 1990s, it was too late for me to go back to my father and ask for more details, to beg him to share with me just one more story. Perhaps I was not destined to. Fortunately, the stories he had told me provided me a trail to follow which took me into the past; a past that consisted of two parallel worlds—one real and one imaginary. The imaginary world was made up of places frozen in my memory, places I had created in my mind as a child while listening to the stories. Going back to revisit them was akin to viewing old damaged frames of a movie. However, one of the places I did visit belonged to the other world and was palpably real. It was a village called Ghasitpura—a village I used to frequent until the mid-1970s, when I was growing up. I also discovered that most of the stories my father had narrated to me, directly or indirectly revolved around a man I never met—Shingara Singh—who hailed from Ghasitpura.

My journey back in time enabled me to re-establish my bonds with his family, which is very special to me, and I learnt how my father's bond with Shingara Singh and his family had inextricably deepened as the result of an incident that took place sometime in 1940s. And so I was able to finally string the precious gems my father bestowed upon me in the correct sequence; a necklace with not a gem out of place.

◆

The underlying narrative of *Bonds of Destiny* is timeless, and reflects a universal truth integral to human consciousness— the need to bond and the desire to connect with people. Communication is the essence of being alive. The coming together of this personal narrative in the form of this book occurred through a coincidental confluence of unrelated events, which has made me a strong believer in the 'connectivity' of happenings in our lives. But it was not until I started writing the preface to this book that I realized that a series of unrelated events or coincidences in my life were in fact linked together through bonds of destiny—bonds we

PREFACE

were destined to create.

◆

I spent the formative years of my life in a small industrial town situated in the north-western Indian state of Punjab. Batala, with a population of about 80,000, lies about 15 miles east of India-Pakistan border, 24 miles north of Amritsar and nearly 350 miles south of Kashmir. During 1970s, it was famed for its foundries and small factories that manufactured all sorts of agricultural equipment and small machines. Buyers from as far as Calcutta (about 2,000 kilometres to the east, and now called Kolkata), and Madras (about 2,700 kilometres to the south, and now called Chennai), would travel all the way to Batala to buy machinery and agricultural equipment.

The archeological history of this town goes back at least five-hundred years to the time of the first Guru of the Sikhs, Guru Nanak. In 1487, nineteen-year old Guru Nanak's wedding ceremony was solemnized in Batala. A crumbling mud wall built close to where the wedding of the first Sikh Guru took place five centuries ago still stands as a testament to the uncanny happenings of the times of the Guru. And I used to visit that wall which, hoary with antiquity, has become a place of worship. Followers of the faith have entombed it and built a majestic Gurudwara at the site named Kandh Sahib (The Holy Wall).

In addition to Guru Nanak, there are many others who earned for Batala a hallowed status. One in recent times was Shiv Kumar 'Batalvi', a college drop-out from Batala. Thanks to his poetry and contribution to the Punjabi language and literature that anyone who speaks Punjabi knows who he was. His pen name 'Batalvi' means someone rooted in Batala.

Growing up in a small town, such as Batala, where my father was a well-known and a much sought-after member of the community, was a mixed blessing. I was expected to conduct myself appropriately whenever outside the house. At the same time, it also gave me immense opportunities to interact with my father's circle of friends and associates, most of whom were influential people in this small town. These individuals included local government officials, doctors, prominent rich industrialists, and the Principal of the only college in town at the time—a college that began as an elementary school run by the Christian missionaries in 1872, and later came to be known as Baring Union Christian College. I was educated there in the mid-1970s, and poet Shiv Kumar 'Batalvi' had dropped out from there in the mid-1950s to devote his time and energies to romantic literature.

As a young boy growing up during the mid-1960s, I had the fortunate experience of knowing Shiv Kumar as the 'poet uncle'; not that I called him that. Every year, just like many families, my family also had a few occasions when my father, his friends and their families would get together for dinner parties that would go on late into the night. My father and his friends would ride the chariot of Bacchus and in quite a few of these gatherings Shiv, the poet uncle, would be present as well. On the insistence of many and at my father's request, he would just recite or resonate a couple of his poems, or nazms, as a valedictory note. While singing his nazms, Shiv would be staring down at nothing and tears would trickle down his eyes. He would not be able to speak any more. His silence spoke for his pain.

Though I could not fully understand his poetry, nevertheless, this was my introduction to the poetry of pathos. By the early 1970s, this interest in nazms transformed itself into my plunge into the poetry of Gulzar, one of the most respected and admired creative geniuses of modern India, a poet, a lyricist, script-writer, movie producer and director, all in one. From the late 1960s through the mid-1980s when I left India, I was deeply influenced by his poetry, most of which I enjoyed through the songs he would write for Indian movies. The imagery in his songs was something anyone could relate to.

A little later in the mid-1970s, a new singer hit the Indian musical scene, Jagjit Singh. He wove the lyrics of contemporary poets into melody, wrapped them in his rich baritone voice and decorated them with the guitar, violin, the Indian percussion instrument 'tabla', and other musical instruments of the day, and presented the ensemble to music lovers. His albums and his music struck a chord with millions. He became an overnight sensation, releasing one album after another, each beating a selling record. For me, his rendition of ghazals offered an ideal balance of three things: deep, yet simple and easy to understand poetry; relaxing light music; and a hypnotic, magical voice that many called beatific and divine. During 1976 through 1981 my college days echoed with the music of this master of the ghazal.

In the summer of 1984, I left India for the US in pursuit of higher education, leaving a part of me far behind, or so I then thought. During my two-plus student years at Oxford, Ohio (1984–1986), I was rather fortunate to see legends of Indian music perform live to a relatively small audience. These legends included Pandit Ravi Shankar, Ustad Zakir Hussain, Pandit Hariprasad Chaurasiya, and Pandit Shiv Kumar Sharma. I did not have the luxury and the pleasure of attending such events in or anywhere near Batala, the town where I grew up. My exposure to live performances was limited to annual events in my high school or family gatherings where the poet uncle would entertain those present.

After finishing the MBA programme in December 1986, I moved to Los Angeles, a large urban metropolis that now boasts a sizeable Indian population, and is one of the biggest markets for Indian artists who come to North America to perform in live shows and concerts.

Beginning from the mid-1980s, Jagjit Singh was in high

demand and started visiting North America for concerts almost every year. His US tour itinerary always included Los Angeles, and I could ill afford to miss his live concerts, set as they were in the ethereal ambience that he created.

In the spring of 1994, not too long after I got married, Jagjit Singh was to perform in front of a gathering of approximately a hundred music lovers. It was a small group of Jagjit Singh's fans. The event was put together by someone I knew, and I was not going to miss this opportunity! It was at this closed-door event that I got a chance to introduce myself and my wife Arti to one of the musicians, in the small group of six musicians accompanying Jagjit, his lead percussionist—tabla player Abhinav Upadhyay. We had a small chat followed by an exchange of phone numbers, a fond highlight of the evening for my wife Arti and me.

Over the years, that brief introduction and a casual exchange of phone numbers grew into an expansive kinship, which came with a mutual liberty to lean upon each other's shoulders when either of us felt down and gloomy—though only over the phone and through frequent exchange of letters. The distance between the two continents did not prevent us from forming a deep tie that soon extended between the two families, mine and Abhinav's.

Now Arti and I would look forward to Jagjit Singh's concert tour to North America because it would enable us to catch up with our friend Abhinav. During his short stays with us, Abhinav would also get a welcome break from his gruelling schedule stretching over thirteen consecutive weeks. He would get to relax in our home—for him a 'home away from home'. It was the spring of 2009 when Abhinav was visiting us and I had just finished the first detailed outline of *Bonds of Destiny*. At the time it was meant only to be a personal narrative that I wanted to document for my two children. A spiral-bound, unedited draft lay on the counter that demarcated the boundary between our open kitchen and our living room. 'What is this brother?' Abhinav asked, 'Can I see it?'

'Of course you can,' I replied, 'this is something that I have been working on for almost twenty years. I started it as a small project and over the years it has evolved into a good-sized personal narrative. You could call it a collection of true incidents chronicled as a story.' And I joked with him, sharing an old adage, 'Three things, wise men say, cannot be kept at home for long—food, daughter and a story', adding, 'a story is meant to be shared, otherwise it is not a story; it is a secret. I think it makes an easy read; you should be able to finish it in about two hours.' This was early in the morning, before I left for work.

Later in the day, when I returned home from work, Abhinav did not ask me if what all he had read during the day was indeed true, because he knew it was. The previous night my wife and I had shared with him pictures from our family visit to India in December 2008; a visit that had included a brief stay with Abhinav in Mumbai. But more significantly, with regard to my spiral-bound narrative, we had shared pictures of our visit with a very special family in Ghasitpura, that hallowed village on the outskirts of Batala, which had held such a key place in my father's stories. Abhinav asked me if I would make him a copy of my spiral-bound material. I gave him the original, letting him know it was a work in progress. This was on Friday, 24 April 2009—two days before my daughter's ninth birthday, a day before Abhinav was to be on stage with Jagjit Singh for a live show in Los Angeles.

I vividly recall Abhinav safely placing the spiral-bound first outline of *Bonds of Destiny* in his briefcase and saying, 'brother, when the time is ripe, I would like to share this story with someone very special; someone who, I know for sure, would have a great appreciation for this unbelievable saga.' I didn't know who he was talking about, but it turned out to be one of the numerous coincidences I mentioned earlier. He shared that first semi-finished, unedited, detailed outline of *Bonds of Destiny* with my hero Gulzar Sahib. But that is another story!

# An Act of Faith

MY PATERNAL grandfather, Satya Dev, had a large family to support. A British government employee in colonial India in the early 1900s, Satya Dev was Headmaster of a middle school. The eighth of ten siblings, my father Bhushan was born in 1924 in the city of Multan, Pakistan. Known as the city of mangoes and citrus fruit, Multan lies about 250 miles southwest of Amritsar that sits on India's border with Pakistan on the west.

My father's older brother Prabodh—nearly thirteen years older—was a staunch nationalist, a freedom fighter, a supporter of India's Independence movement. The local community loved him. India's colonial masters saw him as a radicalized, misguided young man who professed and practised a militant ideology championed by another young nationalist leader from Calcutta, Subhash Chandra Bose. Headmaster Satya Dev, the sole bread-earner of a large family, saw Prabodh as an irresponsible family-member who did not care that his father's ability to support the family depended upon his employment as a Headmaster by the British government. In the eyes of my father, Prabodh was a giving elder brother, someone who had a big heart and one who was always full of surprises.

I remember my father recalling how he got up one morning and found quite a bit of money under his pillow. Since it was more than what his father had given him in the previous three months combined, he realized Prabodh had visited the night before. This was the relationship between my father and Uncle Prabodh while they were growing up.

My father found his father usually upset about Prabodh's adventures and his perilous loyalties to the cause of India's independence, worrying that one day, his anti-British activities would cause Headmaster Sahib to lose a respectable, well-paying government job and face in the community. And then how would he sustain his family and discharge his responsibilities, the most important of which was to marry off his daughters? My grandfather lived with a lingering fear that one day it was all going to be over for him. And it would all be due to Prabodh, a son charting his own territories.

## AN ACT OF FAITH

Uncle Prabodh was a fearless young man with a fire for freedom in him—a fire that could not be doused. He believed that he was a born fighter, and he must fight until his last breath. He believed that foreign rulers were India's enemies, who had been occupying his motherland for centuries, frightening Indians with force and cunning. Since this was the land of Indians, it was his duty as a patriotic Indian to oust foreign occupiers with every possible means. He believed that the only way to oust the British was to use force. To him, Gandhi's non-violent movement was too feeble to achieve anything and therefore, almost inconsequential.

My father vividly recalled one particular conversation between my grandfather and Uncle Prabodh: 'My son,' said grandfather, 'if you keep up with such activities, one day I will definitely lose my job. Your behaviour is absolutely against the interests of our family. Imagine, if I am thrown out, who will keep the wolf at bay? Who will support the family and take care of everybody?'

'You are loyal to your family; I am loyal to my country,' replied Uncle Prabodh, 'I am not trying to be disrespectful, father, I am simply trying to be truthful.'

And my father was left to wonder whether loyalty ought to be defined as loyalty to a cause, to an idea, to a belief? Or should loyalty be defined as loyalty to responsibilities, to commitments, to obligations?

This was the first time my father had heard Uncle Prabodh

firmly but respectfully explaining his priorities to Headmaster Sahib, his father. It was also the first time my father began thinking how his past had influenced his own priorities in life. He was only five years old when he lost his mother with no woman in the family who could transform a house into a home. Headmaster Satya Dev was saddled with the burden of constant worry about money and household responsibilities, the most important of which was marrying off his daughters into respectable families. Little Bhushan constantly felt neglected like an abandoned child in his own home, someone without a family while living with his own family.

A victim of an imaginary homeland, he wanted escape—an escape to Byzantium, where he could ride his own chariot. The colonial hegemony, his family circumstances, and personal aspirations instilled in him a resolve to define his relationship with the world and those around him. He often pondered his destiny and his future, as his present was in disarray. He would often think of his father's life, the life of Headmaster Satya Dev, a disciplined teacher who had followed a noble profession and who had earned a high social standing in the community. And despite his conflict with his son, Headmaster Sahib was proud of Prabodh's leadership qualities and the cause for which he was fighting. Due to fear of retaliation from the government, Headmaster Satya Dev could not openly condone his son's active participation in the militant movement to oust the British. Headmaster Sahib was not colonized, but still not free.

By the time he was eighteen, Uncle Prabodh was leading fiery student protests against the British. He organized a students' movement that eventually led to his election as the founding president of the Multan Students' Union. The winds of student awakening started blowing north and east along the river Ravi, culminating in Lahore. Uncle Prabodh had developed a close association with the Lahore Revolutionary Party.

All of this I learnt through my father's sharing of stories. He was very good at spinning a story within a story and at times I would feel he had wandered off a bit too much and had begun talking of something else altogether. And just when I thought what he was talking about was not connected with the original story, he would surprise me by adding another incident that would beautifully tie the two stories together. Like a skilful carpet-weaver, my father was able to weave a multi-coloured tapestry with so many colourful threads, yet not leave any knots. It was as though the whole mosaic was woven with one single piece of multi-coloured thread.

Just like the stories he passed on to me, where everything in the end would always come together—so was the spread of his life. In the end, everything came together for him. Perhaps this was because he was a resilient man, giving all he had for what he believed in, or perhaps it was because he was destiny's blue-eyed child. I remember him lulling me to sleep:

'Those were the days of freedom struggle, my son. I would think about Gandhi, the apostle of ahimsa (non-violence); satyagraha (fasting on to the truth at any cost, even at the cost of your life); about non-cooperation; and civil disobedience. And I would contemplate my own inward struggles. At times, life did not seem to hold much promise for me. Surrendering before the Lord, my caring deity seemed to be my only option. For me, the essence of life was and continues to be—giving the best of yourself in whatever you do and accepting the outcome, destiny, with as much humility as you have in you. I developed a strong belief that we need to be brave enough to face our true self without questions, without judgments. I wanted to liberate myself from my anxieties to exorcise the demons within. My deep interest in academics saved me from peripheral living. I used to love reading. Any spare moment I had I would read. But all that reading, all that knowledge made me disillusioned. Books gave me a lot of information, but they did not provide me any answers—the answers I was looking for.

In 1939, World War II broke out. The leaders of India's freedom movement were focused against Hitler and the forces of Fascism, but did not want to support Britain and the Allied Forces unless India was assured independence. In 1942, Mahatma Gandhi launched the Quit India Movement and the British agreed in principle to leave India after the war was over. It was around that time that I decided to leave home and join the British Army. I found a way, a way of my own that was different from that of my father and my brother Prabodh, to keep the wolf at bay.

Now my life was full of action. It felt to me at the time I was doing something meaningful. I was responding to the call made by Gandhi, to support the British in their fight against the alliance between Japanese and the Germans. Joining the pack of wolves became a patriotic thing to do. Besides, I figured that joining the army would not only make me financially independent, but also give me an opportunity to do something totally different. Accepting my destiny meant absence of any conflict; conflict between what I had in the present moment versus what I had longed for. It also meant accepting the fact that, like my father, I was going to be another slave to the ruling master!

My faith in life always kept me moving forward. I did not brood much over my past. In the beginning, my life in the army was physically demanding. However, that did not last long. After a short training course, my unit was deployed on the Burma front. That is where British forces supplemented by Indian soldiers were fighting against the Japanese who were aligned with the Indian National Army (INA) under the leadership of Netaji Subhash Chandra Bose. The country was united in the goal—total independence for India. However, our leaders were divided on how to achieve that goal. Mahatma Gandhi, the living embodiment of non-violence, wanted India to join the British in their fight against Hitler. There were others who wanted to fight against Britain and align themselves with the Japanese.

My pensive moods took me to occasional writing. I would write anything that came to my mind. I would write what I felt—the happenings in my life, a life that was turning out to be quite an eventful one. There were strangers around. The country was calling from miles away. Home appeared much nearer than the country, sometimes. I was living in a time of uncertainty and confusion, which is apparent in the notes I had been writing to myself:

> These rulers are holding the sway—day and night! Gandhiji is fighting a losing battle, perhaps. Home is left behind, and so are all near and dear ones. On this island, life has its own contours and its own silhouette. One can neither climb nor descend. I am on an island but I am not an island. Where do I belong? That is my dilemma. Do I belong to my family? Do I belong to my country, my men or this regiment? I am not sure, this is my destiny perhaps, not to know—where, how and why!

Although I was soon promoted to the rank of a junior officer, it had more to do with my command over English language rather than the duration of my service in the army.'

◆

## AN ACT OF FAITH

Life in the army gave my father the opportunity to associate with people from many parts of India—Marathas and Gujaratis from the west, Jats and Rajputs from the deserts of Rajasthan, Dogras from the valley of Kashmir, people from the south, Hindus and Sikhs from Punjab, and then there were Pushtoon and Pathans from the fiercely independent regions of Afghanistan. And there were many other lambs and lions. They all fought alongside each other in the same army for the same cause.

Most of these soldiers back home had seen a little of their vast country, a Babel of different tongues and tribes, a sanctuary for religions from all over the world, teaming with divergent castes and creeds. These soldiers lived with the memories of scenes and smells of their village homes—mud huts, half concealed among palm and banyan trees. In their minds they saw women carrying brass containers brimming with water; during the monsoon, naked children running about the dusty paths and trails in their village; men in dhotis milking cows and irrigating their sparse patches of land from the well nearby, manoeuvring bulls to pull water out from wells to irrigate their fields.

These soldiers had memories of their elders leaning over the hookah, taking their turn and puffing away the smoke of raw tobacco. They heard mooing of cows and the chirping of birds, until no bird sang. They would recall sharp scents of sandalwood and mud walls, the smoke-blackened thatched roofs and the aroma of mustard flowers. All these men represented the timeless and diverse character of India, the real and eternal.

These men in the army did not think over much about the cause for which they were fighting; their minds grasped more readily the simpler pattern of their local circumstances and the experiences of their personal lives. Momentarily, they forgot that their small corner of the battle-front was not the centre of the world-wide struggle. Of distant events they learned from an occasional letter from home, a newspaper, or from rare voices on the air. They lived in the present, and reminisced through memories of their past. The road into the future wound among dark shadows of the known and the unknowable.

Together, they were all working to defeat the Japanese and their alliance with the Indian National Army led by Subhash Chandra Bose, on the Burma front. However, individually, they were all inspired by their total belief in Mother India's ultimate freedom, when finally, the wolves would be out. However, no one could tell how far ahead that day beckoned.

It took all kinds of men to make an army unit—military professionals and wartime amateurs, some quiet, some suave and charming, and others who might be abrupt, tactless and abrasive. One man looked the regular soldier, while another might resemble a country squire or farmer. The diversity of my father's regiment was reflected in the faith of the soldiers. Some believed in Prophet Mohammed and turned towards Mecca to pray and prostrate themselves on little mats, several times a day. Others believed in horoscopes and ominous spirits. Back home, they made sacrifices to their bliss-bestowing gods: Brahma the creator, Vishnu the preserver, and Shiva the destroyer. They worshipped the monkey god Hanuman, and Ganesha, the god with an elephant's head, and Lakshmi, the goddess of prosperity and wealth. There was goddess Saraswati, who represented intellect, knowledge and wisdom; and Krishna the flute-player and the complete man who summed up the essence of life in the Bhagvad Gita's precepts—Knowledge, Meditation and Action.

Others, though a minority, and mostly from southern part of India, were Christians who met in every sense the common perception of people from South India—darker skin tone, shorter in height; but they spoke better English than non-Christian Indians.

And among all these men from all over the country who had joined the army for a single cause of the total independence of India, there was a soldier from the north-western state of Punjab. His name was Shingara Singh. He was of medium height, about 5'7", a thin but strong man with chiselled features.

As part of his religious tradition, Shingara Singh always carried two items with him—a small copy of his holy book the *Sri Guru Granth Sahib,* and a kirpan, a ceremonial dagger. He was a quiet man who did not like the westernized military attire that every soldier was required to wear. A simple man from a village, Shingara Singh felt more comfortable in his village attire, a long kurta—a full-sleeved shirt with no collars, that was long enough to come down to his knees.

Each morning, Shingara Singh could be seen buffing the four-inch blade of his kirpan murmuring verses from the *Sri Guru Granth Sahib*. This buffing of the kirpan was more of a morning ritual than a genuine act of cleaning, as the kirpan had never been used.

Shingara Singh was Bhushan's orderly, which he pronounced as 'ardali'. A dedicated attendant, he was always at the beck and call of his Sahib. He came from a background that was quite different from that of my father. However, my father saw these as artificial divisions, man-made boundaries, and always showed due respect to Shingara Singh.

My father's association with Shingara Singh lasted over four long and varied years, almost till the end of the World War II—a war in which Indian soldiers had joined in response to a call from Gandhi, and thereafter played a significant role in defeating the Nazis and the forces of Fascism.

Away from home, my father felt marooned, as though alone on an island. He yearned to belong. And since he lived alone, he dreamt alone. His life in the army had provided him some purpose, but his destiny was unchartered. He saw everything, experienced much, yet was not committed to anything worthwhile. He had seen people interested in politics, not fanatically attached to any one party or ideology; even the toadies of the government who called themselves liberal. He was well aware of the upsurge of the nationalist movement at the grass root level. Communal riots, acts of stray mindless violence, Gandhi's Peace March, the Quit India Movement, the Hindu-Muslim marriages out of which another real and eternal India was to be born. He wrote in his journal:

> Connecting the Hindu and the Muslim, the British and the Indian, the village and the city—all shall be well. But it does not appeal to my judgment. The appeal is emotional, and that is where perhaps it touches me. In essence, it is an easy optimism.
>
> When I think of Gandhi, I seem to partially agree with him. The Mahatma says, 'Fear is the first enemy of our peasants'. This is the ground where I strike a chord with Shingara Singh, who is here to support his family just as I am here to support myself and perhaps be able to provide some financial help to my father.
>
> But I, somehow, fail to accept Gandhi's insistence on celibacy, hand-spinning and passive resistance. By training, I am a man of action and to me the Mahatma seems to be full of himself and his spiritual struggles and musings.

> However, I feel a strong affinity with the Quit India Movement led by Gandhi that has swept all over India. Gandhi has brought people out of the pampered adolescence, and transformed their lives from the bondage of orthodoxy to a willingness to struggle and sacrifice for an ideal.

Gandhi had appeared as an idea, a myth, a symbol, a tangible reality and a benevolent human being. His god-like presence was visible nowhere but it could be felt everywhere, in everybody's thoughts and deeds. When Gandhi gave the call for the Swadeshi self-reliance and for boycotting imported goods from England, my father and Shingara Singh secretly burnt British currency as a protest against the British rule. This was a small symbolic gesture that became a living epitome of a bond between two individuals who stood united for a cause both personal and nationalist.

My father saw Shingara Singh as a man grounded in a palpable reality—a down to earth, simple honest man, a villager with humble dreams, a family man, who hardly understood the meaning of ideology, movement, disparity, and exploitation, although his was an exploited family, browbeaten by his own countrymen: the local landlords and money lenders. Yet his family, like millions of others, had accepted what life offered them as their fate, their karma—a result of their actions in their past. They rationalized their own sufferings as a rite of passage to nirvana, salvation and eternal bliss!

It was exactly this type of widely dispersed desperation and despondency that could prompt and trigger a revolution, thought my father. He believed that a revolution had its roots in the fields, the streets, the marketplaces. Revolutionaries were rough, but they rarely had the advantage of higher education as did princes and rulers. The language they used came from the heart, not from the lips. It was rooted in mother's milk, the language of the motherland.

And in the present, my father saw his ardali Shingara Singh as someone always over-brimming with emotive reverence for his Sahib, who was Shingara Singh's god of duty.

The daily routine of both the officer and the ardali in the war-zone, gave them sparse opportunities to spend time with each other, though it was more time than my father would spend with other soldiers. In his down-time, Shingara Singh asked his Sahib as many questions as he could, while my father would write down as much as he could about what he felt, experienced and observed. My father's natural instinct was inner reflection. When Shingara Singh asked him questions, he was afraid he would be unable to do justice to the simple questions that Shingara Singh managed to conjure up.

'Sahib, who is Gandhi?' Shingara Singh wanted to know one day.

'He is our neta, our leader.'

'Shaheed Bhagat Singh was also our neta, wasn't he?'

'Yes,' nodded my father.

'Then who is the *real* neta, our *real* leader?' asked Shingara Singh.

'They are all our leaders.'

'When will Hindustan become azad (independent), Sahib?'

'The war is on. Let's see.'

'These foreigners do not know our language; while even I can understand the import behind the words from a language I do not know.'

'They do understand, but they do not speak it,' my father replied.

'How can they understand our problems?'

'They will never understand them because they do not need to.'

'They hanged Bhagat Singh, Raj Guru, Sukh Dev. They are cruel, Sahib. We need a *Guru ki Fauj*, an army of Holy Warriors, to throw them out.'

'We are only doing our duty, Shingara. We have to survive. You have a family to support. And I want to be able to support myself,' said my father, trying to end the conversation.

At times, my father would relapse into anti-war reveries and think of Thomas Hardy's short poem 'The Man He Killed':

*Had he and I but met*
*By some old ancient inn,*
*We should have set us down to wet*
*Right many a nipperkin!*

'They say when we get independence, we will all be equal,' said Shingara Singh. 'Nobody will be more important than others; our independence will bring with it the equality we all deserve. We all will be our own masters with no one from a foreign land to make us slaves. My village will always be green; the dirt tracks will be paved streets flooded with milk. I will sit on my cot and watch my children play. All those fields will sway with flowers, my fields, my village and my mud-house. Do you ever dream?' he asked my father.

'Only when I am asleep.'

In Shingara Singh, my father saw an innocent dreamer of a free India. He wrote:

> Shingara Singh is a simple villager, an illiterate albeit honest man. The larger issues of life are irrelevant to his day-to-day existence. He knows his limitations, and knows that his service to the cause of India's independence is as humble as that of a squirrel in constructing the mythical bridge to Lanka. Yet he remains content. He overturns no trains, sets fire to no buildings, makes no bombs, performs no acts of destruction with indiscriminate enthusiasm, writes no

demands or graffiti on walls, and shouts no slogans. Freedom would hardly bring him anything. His life in free India will not be transformed—neither Gandhiji nor Netaji will ever touch his being. This simple man has only one single ambition that deals with his life in the present moment—to serve his Sahib in military tradition, devotion and unwavering loyalty. His engagement in life is whittled down to a few questions which I cannot answer with all my education. I feel all the humbler.

In Shingara Singh, I see a new type of hero, simple, elemental and passionate, a true Sikh, a lion. An earthy valiant farmer, who belongs to the martial tradition that today mirrors India's emergence to a new life of self-respect, self-determination and independence—a mirror image of the brave Maharaja Ranjit Singh.

# People Will Get to Read My Story

It was a special day in the barracks, although no special occasion. Meat was going to be served for dinner—a weekly luxury in the war-zone—and rum would be available. Enlisted soldiers as well as officers would drop their guard to mingle. Barriers of hierarchy would be brought down for the evening. Around early afternoon that day things became a little tense when the subject concerning the kind of meat to use—Halaal or Jhatka—came up.

Halaal and Jhatka refer to the way the animal is killed. Halaal is an Islamic tradition of slowly cutting an animal's head with a serrated knife while reciting verses from the holy book, thanking the animal and God for the food. The animal then slowly bleeds to death.

Jhatka is when the animal's head is chopped off at one go. Many non-vegetarian soldiers who did not practise Islam, believed that bleeding an animal to death was cruel and inhumane and refused Halaal meat, just like the believers would eat nothing but Halaal.

The matter was sensitive and debatable and there was a heated discussion where emotions ran high. But some decision had to be reached and the matter settled. As the Officer In-charge of the unit, my father was put on the spot. He took a popular vote and the majority voted for Jhatka meat. It was also agreed that since Jhatka meat would be served this time, on the next occasion it would be Halaal.

Unfortunately, this was not the end of the matter. A soldier who practised his faith rather blindly and perhaps was the least of the believers, cursed my father, hurling insults at him—'mother f….., sister f… …' The other soldiers had to intervene to calm things down. It was nothing more than a minor incident for my father. He knew the soldiers were under a great deal of stress. Being an officer, he kept calm and concluded that a flare up in a unit of fifty soldiers did not need to be blown out of proportion. Tempers of all shades need to be kept under check for smooth functioning of the unit.

The party went on late into the night. The next morning as usual, Shingara Singh brought my father his morning tea and brandy, but was uncomfortably quiet. My father asked him if something was bothering him. Looking deep into my father's eyes, Shingara Singh replied, 'Sahib, yesterday that soldier's behaviour was not soldier-like. We all know that he is the best gun-loader we have. The advances our unit has made would not have been possible if he had not been a member of our unit. However, that is not the way we are supposed to behave with an officer, Sahib. That is not how we are trained.'

'That is all right, Shingara Singh,' my father replied. 'The whole episode is behind us now. Last night, the food was good and rum plentiful; we all had a good time. The matter is closed as far as I am concerned. After all, we all are here for a shared cause—India's independence. Such incidents should not be taken so seriously that they distract us from the greater purpose.'

The rest of the day passed off normally. As an officer my father had certain privileges. One of these was access to a kerosene lamp in the evening hours. Shingara Singh would never fail to light up his Sahib's rooms as the night approached. Having a light in one's abode was a good omen. It symbolized that the dwelling was not abandoned. It also meant that the occupants were prosperous enough to afford a lamp. And in Shingara Singh's frame of thinking, under the circumstances, both these meanings were certainly true. Besides, he also knew that his Sahib enjoyed writing. Lighting the lamp was his humble contribution towards the luxury of writing that his Sahib could enjoy in the war-zone. These moments also allowed both men to further strengthen their bond.

'Whenever you get a chance you are always writing something. What is it that you write, Sahib?' asked Shingara Singh.

'Nothing important, I write about what I have been through in my life so far. I wonder if there is any meaning behind us becoming such close friends. I also write about your loyalty towards me,' replied my father, 'tell me about yourself, Shingara Singh.'

'Sahib what can I say about myself. Compared to you, I am nothing.'

'Shingara Singh, you know me well enough. I believe in the eternal equality of human beings. We all are equal. However, due to the roles we play in our lives, we falsely start believing that one person is better than the other. In reality that is not so. My wants, needs and desires are the same as yours. And that is what makes us all equal, not the roles we play in life. Now tell me your story.'

The simple ardali shared his story, 'My story is like the story of any other poor and illiterate man from village. I hail from a small village in Punjab called Ghasitpura. This village is about a two-hour walk from Batala, or about a full-day's walk from Amritsar, the city of Harimandir Sahib, The Golden Temple. Harimandir, is one of the holiest places of my religion. I am married and I have three children—one son and two daughters. I have a younger brother, Bahadur Singh, who is unmarried. He manages the little patch of land we still have, since most of the land we owned was taken over by local landlords.

Now while I am here in the army, my younger brother is looking after the family of four that I have left behind. I send my brother the money I earn in the army. I never went to school because our village did not have one. The only language I can barely read is Punjabi, many of us also call it Gurumukhi, the Guru's utterances. Since you can speak Punjabi very well, you perhaps already know, it is the language spoken by the people of Punjab, the state of five rivers. And I owe my ability to read a bit of Gurumukhi to one Balwant Singh, who is a Granthi, someone who recites the holy book, the scripture, the word of Guru.'

'Why could you not learn how to write?' my father asked.

'For me, Sahib, it was choosing between learning how to write versus what was expected of me as a young child, which was to help in the fields.'

'If you could write, what would you write about?' my father asked.

'I would like to share with others the dreams I dreamt growing up. I would like to affirm my faith in the sacrifices my Gurus made to protect the unprotected. I would write about your coming in my life in the army; about my desire to be protective of you, just like your brother would have been, had he not been so devoted to the cause of Mother India's freedom. And I would end my story with one question—*If I were to die for someone else, how would others remember me?*'

'Shingara Singh, maybe next time when we get a chance to sit like this, you can narrate your story again and I will write it for you, and it will be written in English, since I do not know how to write in Punjabi. Or if you want, I can write it in Urdu for you.'

'Really, Sahib?', said Shingara Singh, 'Then people will get to read my story.'

The following day, a soldier was discovered to be missing from my father's unit—the same soldier who had yelled insults at my father over the Halaal-Jhatka meat controversy. Everyone wondered why the soldier would leave the unit without permission. A frantic search ensued. An urgent notice was dispatched to his house. Time passed. Days became weeks, and weeks turned into two months. There was still no word.

The missing soldier was not only an outstanding gun-loader, but also an enviable sharpshooter. His sudden disappearance was a big loss to the entire unit. An investigation was launched. Many soldiers from the unit were questioned. All of them corroborated the incident that had occurred the day before the soldier went missing—the heated arguments and the soldier yelling insults at my father.

Shingara Singh's loyalty to his Sahib was legendary in the unit. Equally well-known was his devotion to his faith. But everyone also knew that Shingara Singh was not an aggressive person. On the contrary, he was known to be calm and rather quiet, someone who never had an argument with anyone, and had no past record. Shingara Singh was not the kind of person anyone could imagine being violent. Nonetheless, many in my father's unit believed that if anyone could have a reason to harm the missing soldier, it would be Shingara Singh the ardali.

Events unfolded. Shingara Singh was arrested on suspicion of killing the missing soldier, and my father was interrogated. He was suspected of trying to cover up the premeditated murder of a soldier in his unit. All this when there was no physical evidence that the soldier indeed was dead, and certainly no proof that Shingara Singh was in any way connected with the disappearance. The investigation was prejudicial.

'Is your ardali Shingara Singh loyal to you, Bhushan?' asked the investigating officer.

'Yes, he is.'

'Did he show any signs of aggression after the incident?'

'No, absolutely not.'

'Do you think that Shingara Singh killed the fellow soldier?'

'No.'

'What do you think happened to him then?'

'I have no idea,' my father replied. 'If I knew, we would

not be having this investigation.'

'Do you believe your ardali Shingara Singh is innocent and that he has nothing to do with the disappearance of the fellow soldier?' the officer asked.

'Yes, I do,' asserted my father, who had every reason to believe that Shingara Singh's interrogation had not brought anything to light that would close the matter. If it had, no one would be questioning him. At the same time, he wondered what motive Shingara Singh could have to harm the soldier except for Shingara Singh's loyalty towards his Sahib. My father concluded that if Shingara Singh indeed killed the missing soldier, then for him to confess to anything would be inconsistent with why he may have done anything to the fellow soldier in the first place—to protect his Sahib's honour and respect. He further concluded that the fear of causing shame and humiliation to his Sahib would never lead Shingara Singh to confess to anything—even if he was somehow connected with the disappearance.

Shingara Singh, on the other hand, did not know if his Sahib suspected anything or would say anything that would further reinforce the investigating officer's suspicion that he was somehow connected with the disappearance. In essence, Shingara Singh was not sure of my father's loyalty to him.

The investigation quickly entered its final phase and Shingara Singh and my father were brought face to face. This was the first time that my father had seen Shingara Singh since he had been taken away. His forehead was swollen and blue. His left eye was puffed up. He could barely stand. His hands were free but his ankles were shackled. Clearly, he had been tortured. He was acting defiant and fearless. He did not make eye contact with my father who knew right away that Shingara Singh had not confessed to anything.

The relentless questioning started again. My father was asked again if he knew of anything that could link Shingara Singh with the disappearance of the soldier. 'I have nothing more to say than what I have already said. I do not know of anything that could possibly link Shingara Singh to the missing soldier,' he replied.

Frustrated, the British investigator shouted, 'You Indian bastards, you always protect your own, don't you?'

Shingara Singh did not know English. But he had been around English-speaking officers long enough to understand the general tone and meaning of what was said. He shouted back at the officer in Gurumukhi, 'You firangies (foreigners) may not understand our language but we understand yours. This is not how you are supposed to talk to my Sahib, your fellow officer!' And with his right hand on his kirpan, he lurched towards the British investigator shouting, '*Jo Bole So Nihal... Sat Sri Akal*'.[1] The kirpan that Shingara Singh wore

---

[1]This is a traditional saying used by the followers of Sikhism. The first part of the phrase means 'Whosoever utters [this] shall be fulfilled'; and the second

was not a weapon, but a symbol of his faith in the divine, an integral part of his religion, a symbolic reminder, and a source of inspiration to fight against tyranny with whatever little means and might one possessed.

My father knew that Shingara Singh's aggression was an act of loyalty and reverence towards him, as well as a symbolic act of defiance against the oppressive ruler. He did not mean to harm the investigator, let alone kill him. He had only placed his hand on the kirpan, he had not pulled the knife out of its sheath. However, the justice system of the British Army failed to see it that way. Its investigators were already convinced that Shingara Singh was the man behind the disappearance of the fellow soldier. And now, the 'murder suspect' had attempted to kill the investigator by assaulting him with a knife.

Shingara Singh was charged with assault with a deadly weapon intending to kill an active officer of the British Army. A summary trial followed in which Shingara Singh was court-martialled and sentenced to death by hanging.

My father was exonerated of all charges.

---

part of the phrase is a call for triumph, and victory. Followers of the Sikh faith also use this expression as a way to charge themselves in religious fervour or to express a mood of joy and celebration.

# A Collector of Worlds

THESE WERE trying times for my father. Joining the army and undergoing the events that ensued, turned out to be far more challenging and demanding than he could have ever anticipated. And it all happened in a war zone far away from home. By now my father's nomadic existence had become stressful. Besides, the last conversation he had with Shingara Singh was playing on his mind. Shingara Singh had expressed a desire to tell his story. 'Were I to ghost-write it, what story would I write on my ardali's behalf?' he wondered. He was also haunted by memories of his elder brother Prabodh and his battles. Since there had been no news from home for a long time, he had no idea what Prabodh was up to.

This was the beginning of another chapter in my father's life on his journey from innocence to experience. Cast perhaps in mythical mould, he seems to have been determined 'to strive, to seek, to find and not to yield'. With wanderlust in his blood and the creative urge in his soul, despite having been through a hellish experience, he felt resurrected, believing that the worst was over for him. Now, if only there was a way that he could help Shingara Singh too.

My father not only had a flair for languages, but also a flair for expressing his version of reality; sometimes even creating one. This created reality would naturally be based on what was going through his mind, as a collector of worlds. Although dislocated in time and place, he was not by any measure, out of place. It was as if he had been exiled to a new location, a new freedom, which his home had denied him—a home that he missed terribly. He had not joined army for monetary gain, or for adventure or for reputation. It was an escape. But even now when he looked around there was no one he could call his own. The place was not his own either. Caught up in a kind of existential homelessness, he was desperately looking for an identity, a definitive one. He wanted to reconstruct himself in his thought and quest for experience in new ways, in new understandings, among new people and under new circumstances.

He was one of those individuals who were principally aware of one culture, one setting, and one home. He knew well that his life was in a continuous state of flux—unknown, unseen, unpredictable, without order, without shape, without pattern. Only distance existed. He carried with him the blurring outlines of his past—a story in the making. He believed that life became more meaningful if one dreamt of possibilities, territories unchartered and unexplored.

As an officer in the army, he found his reality at odds with his faith and conviction. He wondered what he could have done to protect his loyal attendant Shingara Singh, his ardali. He questioned his role, as though he questioned 'Is there a life after death?' Perhaps a metaphysical probing!

♦

The monsoon of 1945 had left a trail of misery among the soldiers, and my father became one of its victims when he contracted cholera. His sickness gave his commanding officer a perfect and absolutely a legitimate reason to get rid of him and erase the last memory of the unfortunate episode of the missing soldier, and my father was moved out of the unit and sent to the Army Hospital in Calcutta. Although beset with cholera, my father found the move a welcome reprieve, a break from his dreary existence in the war zone.

So far as his immediate future was concerned, the people who meant the most to him were the doctors, nurses and the support staff. Fortunately for him, they all thought he was someone important, with influential connections. Otherwise how could a non-white soldier be moved out of a combat zone so quickly? The news of his involvement in the recent investigation did not follow him to the hospital. No one knew what he had been through and how his ardali, after being sentenced to death, was now awaiting execution. In order to avoid any further probing, he decided he was not going to volunteer any information either, unless someone specifically asked him.

During the day, he would stay in the bed, resting. At night he would play cards with nurses and other patients he had befriended. As a result of the four or more people that sat on the bed each night to play bridge or some other card game, the joints of his bed were perpetually coming loose, much to the mystification of the maintenance staff. It was never tracked down to him. In fact, my father seemed to have a Midas touch. Wherever he went, small privileges followed him. And his admittance to Calcutta Army Hospital was no exception. The hospital staff went out of their way to take care of this important officer's day-to-day needs. He enjoyed the special treatment and began discovering a new world bubbling with caring individuals. It was in sharp contrast to the violence and killing he had witnessed during the past several years.

Kiran, one of his nurses, was especially kind to him. She possessed the proverbial patience of a nurse. She smiled, she listened and she seemed to understand. Her nurturing nature and fondness for my father encouraged him to share some stories from his personal life with her. He was careful though, not to share anything about the recent events concerning the disappearance of a soldier and the investigation that followed.

He shared with Kiran that his decision to join the British Army was motivated by his desire to get away from home; serving in the British Army during the war was also his way of contributing to the cause of India's independence. He hoped the British would leave India after the war was over. He shared with Kiran that his elder brother Prabodh was fighting for the freedom of the motherland in his own way, even though the British thought that he was a radical, misguided young man who needed to be locked up behind bars.

However, Kiran had also sensed the conflict within my father about being in the army, a conflict that had turned into a tremendous burden. 'One day when history is written, what will they write about me?' he asked, and then shared with her the epitaph he had written for himself: 'Here lies a man who not only sided with foreign occupiers, but also chose to serve his brother's foes; a brother who was considered a fearless revolutionary and for whom the cause of India's independence was the sole purpose of his life. Here lies the soul of a betrayer.'

He spoke to Kiran about Prabodh, 'The Revolutionary in the Family', who had said to his father, 'You are loyal to your family; I am loyal to my country'. Those words that he had heard during Prabodh's last visit and before he left home to join the British Army, were now indelibly engraved in his mind.

◆

One Sunday morning, when the doctors had finished with their rounds for the day, he sat in his hospital bed writing furiously. He was preoccupied with the inevitable events that were going to unfold themselves for Shingara Singh.

At 3.00 p.m., Kiran began her shift. 'Bhushan,' she said, 'your recovery has been unusually fast; all the test results are normal. And even though it will take you some time to feel as energetic as you used to be, we are going to discharge you tomorrow. I know you are not going to be happy to hear this, but I wanted to let you know that you will be asked to report back to your unit.'

Bhushan liked everything he heard except for the last bit. He knew he had recovered from cholera, but the recovery from cholera was just one aspect of his concerns. The other two related to his mental and emotional state. 'I am not at all happy at the prospect of going back to my unit and resuming my services to the colonial masters,' he replied, overcome with emotion. Realizing that this was not the best time to continue the conversation, they decided that time permitting, Kiran would visit him later in the afternoon. Otherwise, she would find some other time to resume the conversation.

My father did not want to go back to the army. He did not know where else he could go either. He wondered if there was any way that his stay in the hospital could be extended. Kiran knew him well, he thought, and she seemed to be fairly understanding of his situation. He could feel her empathy. Perhaps, she could help him to prolong his stay.

His kinship with Kiran had enabled her to learn a great deal about his childhood. She knew that he had lost his mother when he was five, that he was a neglected young child in a large family which made him feel an orphan, a homeless child in his own home. He had even shared with Kiran his vivid memories of the hot summer day in Multan when his mother suddenly died of brain haemorrhage around 11.00 a.m. Bhushan was given the responsibility of informing the neighbourhood. He remembered going from door to door telling families, 'My mother has left us all forever. She will be cremated this evening. Please join us in sharing our grief.' He had confided in Kiran that at that time he did not know what dying meant; however, he did know it was something very sad and that it forever changed the lives of those left behind.

Kiran also knew that Bhushan had once run away from home when he was thirteen during the summer holidays, supporting himself by working at a neighbourhood grocer's shop. Only after his father, Headmaster Satya Dev, persuaded him to come back home, he relented. Kiran also knew that his decision to join the British Army was primarily driven by his desire to escape life at home. Perhaps, it was an attempt to run away from his own self.

The following day, my father again asked Kiran if there was anything she could do to extend his stay in the hospital. It turned out that Kiran's sister Usha had a position of responsibility at a convalescent home that was about five miles away from the Army Hospital. Kiran was able to arrange for his admission. Thanks to her help he was out of the hospital and moved into a convalescent facility meant for patients who needed a longer recovery.

My father thanked her with heartfelt gratitude, 'You are a true "Nightingale" of your profession. I have no words to express my thankfulness and appreciation for what you have done for me. As a devotee of Saraswati, the goddess of knowledge and wisdom, I feel you know that you are wise. I have ambitions but I need repose to contemplate, to reflect, to chew over all that has happened in the recent past. It's not that I want to live in the past,' he said, 'but that past is not going to leave me alone. It is going to follow me like my shadow.'

'My brother, my father, my sisters—where are they all?' he cried, 'I am so poor—a derelict,' my father was overwhelmed.

'Take heart,' Kiran sympathized. 'Everything will fall into place. Time is the greatest healer, it heals all wounds. You will feel better there. At the convalescent facility, they will make you feel at home. I believe you will like it there.' Kiran's words of support, said in her comforting and consoling voice, made my father feel better about himself and hopeful about the future.

◆

In the convalescent home, Usha waited for his arrival. A devoted worker, Usha served with missionary zeal. Twelve years earlier, her husband from seven-month long marriage had died in a tragic road accident. Since that time, she had dedicated herself to this convalescent facility and its occupants.

Usha was not Kiran's biological sister, but an adopted orphan who had been raised by Kiran's parents. My father did not know all this until he met Usha and learnt more about her. Just like him, Usha too had finished two years of college followed by some training that qualified her to work at this facility. In every aspect, this institution was fortunate to have her, and she was lucky to have chosen it as her first job after she became a widow.

My father was unclear about her exact title or position, but she was responsible for the facility's day-to-day operations. She seemed to have earned her authority and respect through her dedication to this facility and its inmates, followed by meticulous attention to detail in whatever she did. She lived on premises in a one-bedroom unit that had a small living room and a kitchenette. Her dwelling was a part of the compound that included eight other units of different sizes. These units were allotted to other members of the staff running the facility. In addition to her job, Usha enjoyed reading Rabindranath Tagore, the famous writer from Bengal who had won the Nobel Prize for Literature in 1913 and had passed away in 1941. Usha had not only read Tagore's original works in Bengali, but also treasured English versions.

My father found comfort in her company. He did not know Bengali and therefore had not read Tagore's original works. However, he had read some translated works of Tagore in high school and college. He shared one of his favourite poems with Usha:

*Where the mind is without fear*
*And the head is held high;*
*Where knowledge is free;*
*Where the world has not been broken up*
*Into fragments by narrow domestic walls;*
*Where words come out from the depth of truth;*
*Where tireless striving stretches its arms towards perfection;*
*Where the clear stream of reason has*
*Not lost its way into the dreary desert*
*Sand of dead habit;*
*Where the mind is led forward by thee*
*Into ever-widening thought and action—*

*Into that heaven of freedom, my Father,*
*Let my country awake.*

With their similar backgrounds and interests, both drew close. Usha had no one she could call her own. And my father was away from home—1,200 miles away in the East, working at the history of his times, his life, his feeling of separation from the rest of the world. They both could relate to each other. Their closeness to each other rejuvenated them both. Both saw hope in their future. Both wondered if they were meant to be a family.

My father had many worlds to explore—his own and those of others. The world had existed for him as an imaginary home created in his mind through longings and fantasies. His thoughts seemed far away, and this was because he himself was trying to find his way in the world. In Usha, he found an eager reader of his memoirs and his notes to himself. In her, he found someone who genuinely wanted to know him. He shared with her a note he had written:

> A person with imagination perhaps has no regrets in life. One has to make choices. I chose the army, chose to serve the masters: for more than one reason and most important of all, for an escape. I had to sacrifice the comfort zone called home, suspend my education to enter the world that was strange, sudden and violent. To live in this world is to live with impressions, sometimes

blurred, sometimes clear. I feel as if I am a pendulum swinging between dream and stark reality. With my brother passionately engaged in the freedom struggle, I only wish I could share his ambitions. We all want a free India, but only a few are determined to fight to the finish. My brother is one of them. I would have been of some help to him, had I too joined the struggle. The struggle has great magnitude. To dislodge the British rulers is not that easy. But it is not impossible either. A new renaissance has been born in my country—Gandhi, Nehru, Bose, Tagore.

Pages from his journal were his best introduction to the people around him and the happenings of his times. During one of their conversations, he shared his impressions about Tagore with Usha. 'Yes, he is as great in music as in poetry. His songs are sung from India to Burma. When he was in sorrow, he wrote beautiful love songs. Then his art became deeper, it became religious and philosophical.'

'What I admire the most about Tagore is the expression of human aspirations in his hymns,' Usha said.

'Moreover, the poet-musician surrenders himself to the spontaneity of the soul,' added my father.

'Yes, it is obvious in his paintings also. At times, I wonder if he has it from the culture of Bengal, from nature, or from the love of God.' Usha could see that Tagore's art and philosophy had deeply impacted my father.

'It is said about Tagore that reading one line by him can help one forget all the troubles of the world,' said my father in a tone that implied that this was the greatest praise that could be heaped on the poet.

◆

The previous three years of his life, my father had chronicled in his fragmented notes to himself and in his journal. These writings gave a peep into his state of mind, his inner tensions and dilemmas, and his feelings about Shingara Singh. The relationship between the officer and the ardali had been tender, deep, sustained and affectionate, and he remembered Shingara Singh with nostalgia and longing. He appeared in Bhushan's reveries as a powerful reincarnation of Raicharan—a character in Tagore's short story titled, 'My Lord, The Baby'.

He nurtured a secret desire to meet Shingara Singh, just one more time and share with him the memories of days gone by. He wanted to experience those mornings and evenings when he connected with someone deeply—just one more time.

Some relationships, my father felt, defy definitions. They exist at subterranean levels and give meaning to human existence. They are an assertion of life, its very justification, and its very essence. My father felt his relationship with

Shingara Singh fell in this category.

One day as she finished reading my father's notes on Shingara Singh, Usha asked, 'Bhushan, where is Shingara Singh these days?'

Although he did not want to go into any details, my father did want to unburden himself to someone, to anyone inclined to listen. 'On death row, in some dark and dingy prison cell waiting to be hanged until he is dead. I do not know where,' he said with frustration. 'He was accused of the attempted murder of a British Army officer who was investigating the disappearance of a soldier in my unit. I have known Shingara Singh for over three years. I knew his dedication to his duties and his total loyalty and commitment to me. I am so distraught by the whole episode that I really cannot talk about this anymore. A man who simply acted to protect his faith and my honour, with no intention to kill anyone, is going to be hanged.'

Usha was dumbfounded and not knowing what to say changed the subject, 'Where is your brother, Bhushan? Are you in touch with him?'

'I read about him in a local newspaper. He was arrested in Punjab, and this time he is being kept in a solitary confinement in Alipore Jail, a high-security prison, less than five miles from here. They have moved him away from Punjab, his home state.'

'I gather he is your ideal. He inspires you in your moments of loneliness, doesn't he?'

'Yes, he does! And I feel so sad when I think of him. A fighter who took the fight on his shoulders, sacrificed all he had. He is a real fighter. I too fought. I fought for the rulers, I fought for our independence in my own way, but against whom? Shingara Singh used to ask me the same question: "Who are we fighting against, and who might we kill?"'

He asked Usha if she could arrange for a typewriter for him. He felt something surging within, which might find expression. Writing his journal whenever he could was an inner necessity, an urge, a cathartic relief. Through writing, he wanted to seek a way into the future, reach out to the next generation. In a typewriter, he would find a companion he thought was loud, living and lasting.

Usha arranged for an old Remington typewriter which had not been used for a while. My father cleaned and oiled his aged, new companion. Now, he could belong to the future, he could extend himself. He knew words had power. He believed energies emanating from words exploded in time and space.

Rising early, thanks to his army background, my father would complete his morning routine, and thereafter keep himself busy with typing and finish what he had started the night before. It was not always easy to organize his thoughts. He was in search of a centre—a master narrative, a metaphor for his life. So far, he had been appropriating the events of his life into a random plot. He knew the future wasn't there yet, neither was there a proper beginning. There was only this middle—a dynamic relationship of ends and beginnings, and a kind of process that only constitutes the middle. He echoed his musings:

> 'I don't know what it is. I don't know whether I'm worrying or not, whether I can or not; whether I can cry or not. I am like a wet seed sown in hot earth. I live in false times. Truth will visit me only when I am among my own people. There is a world beyond, which I must acknowledge and touch one day. Today, it is all blurry—an illusion.'

He recalled what Shingara Singh had said, quoting the first Guru of his faith, Guru Nanak, and Bhushan translated the hymn into English.

> *He deprives of delusion*
> *The things that delude*
> *He blunts the edge of the dagger*
> *And it does not wound*
> *Man's mind wavers for it is full of craving*
> *He is safe only in the Lord's keeping.*

This particular morning, with tired fingers, he continued typing for more than four hours. It was a struggle against the self and against the world that was taking shape around him. The moment of arrival was far, far away.

Thoughts of Halaal meat and Jhatka meat flashed across his mind. Again, the dichotomy brought to his mind Guru Nanak's hymn:

*A Muslim's faith is to follow the Prophet*
*Caring neither for life nor death,*
*To accept the Ordinances of God,*
*To believe He is the One and the Only Creator*
*And obliterate every thought of self.*

He was loading up a fresh page in the typewriter when he heard distant footsteps in the hallway. It was rather early. Who could it be? It could not be Usha as she usually visited at fixed hours. Then he heard a knock on his door and opened it. A white woman accompanied by Usha and a few soldiers stood outside.

Usha made the introductions. 'Officer, this is Lady Reid, visiting recovering soldiers to thank them for their services.'

'Lady Reid, this is Bhushan, an officer with the Fifth Division. His was an acute case of cholera. He was shifted here straight from the Burma front. He is recovering slowly. Full recuperation is going to be a slow and a long process.'

My father, who had been immersed in typing for a while stood dazed, not knowing how to react or what to say. The fact that while introducing him to Lady Reid, Usha had addressed him as 'Officer' did not go unnoticed. He stood aside as Lady Reid entered the room followed by Usha and the soldiers.

Lady Reid quickly surveyed the room. It was most unlike a typical patient's room. Scattered typed-written pages carried the mark of a writer's agony. She picked up a page, read a few lines, looked at my father and said, 'You seem to be a writer in the making. To write about oneself is perhaps the most difficult. Tell me Officer, suppose you were stranded on a deserted island, which book would you like to have with you?'

My father thought over the question for a few seconds and then said, 'The Oxford English Dictionary.'

Lady Reid looked at him in some disbelief, holding a page from the discarded bunch.

> Despite our age difference, I feel so close to my brother Prabodh. We never spent much time together. He was always passionately devoted to the cause of freedom. With my brother seldom at home, I hardly had a chance to get to know him. My bond with him is so very special. He is as near as father is distant. What an irony! We never had a heart-to-heart talk. I know more about my own brother from others—that he is a nationalist, a freedom fighter. He dreams of a free India, an India where there are no rulers and where all are equal. Free India! Our own India! How intensely I long to see him. For long I have not seen him, have not heard from him.

Having read the page, Lady Reid sat down on my father's bed and asked him to sit down next to her. The accompanying entourage was in a state of shock; it did not expect this to happen. My father did not know what to make of it. She insisted he tell her more about his brother Prabodh. Her concern was evident in the way she spoke. And it was this compassion that enabled my father to feel at ease.

Lady Reid did not need to hear about the closeness of their relationship. It was obvious to her from the page she just finished reading. My father then shared some pertinent facts about Prabodh's situation with Lady Reid and ended with one final desire, 'He is less than five miles from here, yet he is far, very far away. I wish there was a way I could meet my brother.'

'I am indeed touched by your honesty and what you have written in these pages. I cannot promise you anything, but one thing I do promise is that I will do my best to help you meet your brother.'

Pain brings its own balm. My father felt consoled. In his mind he saw his brother in handcuffs, face unshaven, ruffled hair, dreamy eyes; dressed in white khadi kurta-pyjama. He was in a cell all alone, by himself. Sunlight came in from a narrow window high on one of the walls. You could not see any sky, though. Alone, he waited for a new dawn. Waiting for the long night to be over, reminding himself, '*Kahin to hoga shab-e-sustmauj ka sahil; kahin to ja ke rukega safina-e-gham-e-dil.* (Somewhere is the verge of night's slow-washing tide; somewhere is an anchorage for the ship of heartache).

He woke up with a sudden jerk. The dream had vanished. My father was alone again. A soldier on the horns of a dilemma—attached and detached at the same time. In search of solace after years of constant fight and fatigue. He had been exposed to the vagaries of colonial hegemonic ambivalences at a very young age, which his elder brother had taken upon himself to resolve. My father felt a chasm separating the two, creating an uncanny distance which he longed to bridge with real proximity.

It was Usha's final round for the day. She felt sorry that she had not been able to alert my father about Lady Reid's visit ahead of time, although she herself did not know that Lady Reid would be visiting that day. She told my father who Lady Reid was, 'She is the wife of a very senior British officer and takes a keen interest in the welfare of soldiers. As a matter of fact, she is the Honorary Chairperson of the Army Officers' Welfare Organization. In that role, she visits hospitals and other facilities such as this one, to thank soldiers for their service and to see if she can be of any help. She is a very nice person. I have known her for three years now and I have every reason to believe that she will do everything she can to help you, especially if she has told you so.'

◆

It was Tuesday. At around 11.00 a.m., Ram Chand, the peon,

knocked on the half-open door. My father looked up and Ram Chand relayed his message, 'Sir, Usha Madam wants to see you in her office.'

'You may let her know Ram Chand that I will be there shortly,' he replied. He was surprised. What could the matter be? Was his stay in the Home over? Were they going to ask him to leave? His mind was racing with a gnawing sense of fear and apprehension. 'The matter must be official. Why else would I be asked to come to see her in the office?' he asked himself. As he entered the office, Usha seated behind her desk asked him to take the chair across her.

'Excuse me for bothering you,' she said. 'There is good news for you, Bhushan. Lady Reid has sent her car to pick you up.'

'To pick me up?' He was astonished.

'Yes, to pick you up. You are going to see your brother today.'

He looked at Usha in utter disbelief. 'I am?'

'Yes, you are. Now please get ready to go. Today is a special day. The car will first take you to Lady Reid's residence. There she will be joining you. And together you are going to Alipore jail. I can tell that Lady Reid has made the necessary arrangements.'

Usha had cheered up his spirits. His heart was filled with joy. He was ecstatic. What more could he ask? In great excitement, he ran back to his room, stuffed his bag with his journal, some loose papers that carried his notes, and a pen. In no time, he was back in Usha's office, all set, and ready to go.

Lady Reid's residence was not too far and the driver was pulling into the long driveway of a colonial bungalow in about fifteen minutes. My father was led by a staff member dressed in white to a small waiting room, adjacent to a huge living room. The wait was not too long. Lady Reid soon entered with one of her assistants following. 'Sit down, please, Bhushan,' she said in her tender voice. 'You know today you will get to see your brother. All necessary arrangements have been made. Before we go and visit him, you must get something for him, I suppose. What does he like the most?'

'Rasgullas and mangoes,' replied my father without even thinking.

Both items were procured and arranged in a basket. Lady Reid carried a nice bouquet of flowers. They drove to Alipore jail in her official car. My father was lost in thought, 'I wish all rulers were like Lady Reid, above petty racial and ethnic considerations, with faith in basic human goodness, believing in cultural affirmation, integrity and harmony. How lucky I must be to have that first encounter with Lady Reid. Was it me or was it that one page that she read. Or perhaps it was meant to be, pre-destined. I am not sure. For me Lady Reid does not represent the ruling British elite. She is just a very kind woman who tries to relate to people and who wants to connect two brothers. Her gesture though simple, and not grandiose, is still so powerful. I think it is an effortless acknowledgement of the dedicated struggle of Indians towards freedom.'

Elated at the prospect of seeing his brother, my father's thoughts were transformed into lyrical musings, almost a poem:

> *We are dreamers*
> *In search of floating gardens*
> *Eluding us*
> *We*
> *The chasers of un-harvested orchards*
> *In search of our own land*
> *Our own home*

The car came to a smooth halt. The driver, a Sikh, got out and quickly opened the door for Lady Reid. Lady Reid walked in accompanied by my father, an Indian. The jail staff was taken aback. This was something unusual and unexpected. My father must be a very special person, they all surmised. Lady Reid walked into the office of the jail Superintendent and asked for prisoner Prabodh Chandra. The driver carried the basket with mangoes and rasgullas. Lady Reid handed the bouquet of flowers to my father, sending a message to the Superintendent that the flowers were not meant for him!

◆

My father had chosen fresh mangoes, as he knew Uncle Prabodh liked them very much. Even I have a very vivid memory of an encounter with my uncle that revolves around his love for the king of all fruits. It was the summer of 1978, and I was visiting New Delhi. I decided to visit my uncle. At the time he was a Member of Parliament, representing District Gurdaspur in Punjab. He lived in a bungalow allotted to him.

It was a hot afternoon, and I was in a taxi, driving along the long wide boulevards where once upon a time, British officers used to live in the palatial bungalows on either side. Now the same bungalows were occupied by the Members of Parliament, senior bureaucrats and ministers running the India of the late 1970s. One of these palatial bungalows—18 Janpath—was the official residence of my uncle. I arrived. There was a watchman who asked me who I was and that was it, I was let in. The front lawn was very well kept. The property had huge trees on it, trees that had outlived the original occupants of the place—the ruling elite of India of pre-independence times.

I entered the living room, a huge one. Its walls were adorned with oil paintings of freedom fighters by a well-known studio named Chitrashala. Most of these leaders I had learned about during my formative school years.

A staff member who had been with my uncle perhaps for thirty years recognized me. He offered me cold water and asked if I would like to have lunch. It was around two in the afternoon. I let him know that I was there to simply see my uncle. He informed me that my uncle was resting in his bedroom but he was not taking a nap. I told the staff member that I would wait for my uncle. He asked me where my luggage was, assuming that I would be spending at least a couple of nights there. I told him that I was there just to see my uncle, how he was doing and that was all.

As we were having this conversation, I saw my uncle walking in. It was my good fortune that he was there on that day, at that moment. It was one of those rare encounters I had with him when he was not surrounded by people. As always, he was walking slowly, taking each step deliberately. He was wearing crisp white hand-spun khadi kurta-pyjama, the 'unofficial uniform' of almost all Indian politicians with nationalist ideologies and leanings.

Indian politicians wore it then and they wear it even now. They started wearing this uniform way back in the 1920s in response to a call made by Mahatma Gandhi, who had asked Indians to unite and boycott imported cotton cloth manufactured in the mills of England.

The British were importing raw cotton bought from poor Indian farmers at rock bottom prices, feeding it into their cotton mills and fuelling the British economy. The finished product—imported machine-made fabric—would come back to India and compete against hand-spun cotton made in villages and small towns of India. Local producers could not compete against the cheaper imported cloth and this destroyed the economy of India at the grass-root level.

Today this khadi uniform of the politicians is perhaps their only connection with the masses, seventy per cent of whom still live in the villages, with no access to running water and other necessities of life. But Uncle Prabodh belonged to a different generation of politicians who had been associated with Mahatma Gandhi and India's first Prime Minister, Nehru since the 1940s. For him, wearing hand-spun cotton was more than just a demonstration. It was a way of life, perhaps his way of connecting with the common man.

And in the present, here he was, Uncle Prabodh walking towards me. I immediately got up and bowed to touch his feet seeking his blessings. He held me by my shoulders and asked me to sit down. I waited for him to sit down first. Then I pulled a chair from dining room area and sat next to him.

'How is Bhushan?' was his first question.

'Uncle, he is doing fine. How is your health?' I asked in return.

'I have to watch my blood pressure. Other than that, I am in good health.'

Then, all of a sudden, we were interrupted by the doorbell. Uncle looked towards the door. The watchman, the same person who had ushered me in, came in and asked my uncle if he should let in a fruit seller who had brought fresh mangoes.

'The man is insisting that Sahib had asked him a few days ago to stop by whenever he had a good selection of ripe mangoes,' said the watchman.

Though age had slowed my uncle a bit, he remained very alert. He spoke very softly, almost whispered, by habit and by the same token had equally good hearing abilities. He had overheard the conversation softly told the watchman to get the fruit seller in.

The man was duly ushered in carrying a basket full of mangoes on his head. This was his chosen selection. He had hand-picked them and set them aside while he made door-to-door calls on these luxurious homes. Now he asked uncle how many kilos he wanted.

'How much do you have in this basket?', asked uncle.

'I do not know Sahib,' said the man, 'maybe about 25 kilos.'

'So how much is it?'

The man had a bewildered look on his face. He had not expected my uncle to buy the whole basket. 'Sahib, it would be seventy rupees.'

My uncle took out a roll of notes from the breast pocket of his kurta, and handed the man a hundred-rupee note. The fruit seller started scrambling for change nervously; clumsy and in a hurry to get out of there. Very politely, my uncle requested the fruit seller to keep the change. The man did not understand. He was not used to such a generous tip. When people told him to keep the change, it meant a few coins not rupees. Such was my uncle. Not only did he not bargain with the fruit seller, but he also offered him a very generous tip.

Uncle Prabodh asked a staffer to have some of those fresh mangoes served up. He wanted everyone present—cooks in the kitchen, the attendant, the watchman, and the fruit seller—to enjoy the seasonal fruit. In that sense, he was very respectful to his staff.

In almost no time, freshly cut mangoes with chilled sweetened milk were waiting for us on the dining table. My uncle seemed to relish this seasonal fruit with gusto. And for me, those were the best mangoes I ever remember eating in the company of an important person, a fiery nationalist, a visionary, who never dropped his ordinary self even when he held positions of importance.

♦

Lady Reid's driver was holding the basket with mangoes and rasgullas, while she was having a conversation with the jail Superintendent. Instead of getting the prisoner out, Lady Reid demanded they be allowed to visit the prisoner in his cell. And that is what happened. The Superintendent showed the way and Lady Reid, holding my father's hand, led him to Uncle Prabodh's prison cell.

Uncle Prabodh had no clue that he was going to have visitors. He saw a white woman whom he neither recognized nor knew. He had not seen his younger brother for years either, and therefore had a look of total disbelief in his eyes. The two brothers hugged and cried. The Superintendent, assisted by his subordinates, tried to separate the two. Lady Reid almost yelled at the Superintendent and demanded that he along with his staff leave the prison cell. 'Here are two brothers meeting after years, just leave them alone!' That was enough for them to leave the cell, although with hesitation.

Lady Reid then introduced herself to Uncle Prabodh as a social worker, adding that she gave most of her time to Army Officers' Welfare Organization. She further explained that during her visit to the convalescent facility, she had met his brother Bhushan who was recovering from a severe attack of cholera, and had seen something he had written. It was a powerful piece of writing that had touched her heart and soul, she said. She also mentioned to Uncle Prabodh that she knew someone who had made her visit to the cell and the meeting possible.

My uncle was greatly touched by her thoughtful gesture and thanked her for her time and effort and above all, her caring approach that made this meeting of two brothers possible. He also joked with Lady Reid, 'If it was my home, I would have served you some hot tea, and welcomed you with the traditional Indian hospitality. In our culture, a guest is God in disguise. However, in this jail, I cannot offer you anything more than what you have very kindly brought for me—seasonal mangoes and rasgullas. Most importantly, by bringing my baby brother to me you have demonstrated that even rulers can feel for their subjects.'

Lady Reid looked at him and said that it was because of what she had read in the page that his baby brother had typed, and that had led to everything. Then she left the cell, leaving the two brothers alone, and informed my father that she would be waiting outside, in the courtyard, in the shadow of a tree that had a bench under it.

The meeting of two brothers lasted for about an hour. During the meeting, my father discovered the 'crime' for which his brother had been sent to Alipore Jail. Uncle Prabodh told him that after Subhash Chandra Bose successfully escaped despite British surveillance on his house in Calcutta in 1941, he made his way to Russia through India's North-West Frontier with Afghanistan. He had journeyed to Peshawar with the help of the Abwehr, a German military intelligence/information-gathering organization. On his way to Peshawar, Subhash Chandra Bose had spent a night in Lahore, in the same safe house that Uncle Prabodh had been using for a long time and which the police also suspected that he used.

One of the family members in the house was a lady named Sawraj, who recognized Subhash Chandra Bose and insisted he autograph a picture that had appeared in the newspaper alongside the news announcing his escape. A few days later, there was a police raid on the house and they found the newspaper with Bose's autograph. This gave the authorities enough evidence that Uncle Prabodh had a hand in facilitating Bose's escape to Russia.

Prabodh also told Bhushan how an elderly member of the jail staff alerted him to a plot to kill him: an undercover British operative would be introduced in the prison cell and he would lure Prabodh into a police-hatched 'escape plan' that would result in a police shootout, killing him. Though he thwarted that plan, within the next week or so he was banished to the Andaman and Nicobar islands in the southeast of India. The British were using them as an isolated penal colony for members of India's Independence movement.

I also remember my father telling me that he was able to share all that had happened with his ardali Shingara Singh since the disappearance of a soldier in his unit. He told his brother everything that he knew had happened, and everything he thought *might* have happened. He also informed Uncle Prabodh how Shingara Singh had been sentenced to death for a crime that he had never committed.

On the lighter side, my father told me that both brothers enjoyed the rasgullas and the mangoes together to their hearts' content. That meeting between the two brothers ended on a positive note, my uncle getting Lady Reid's permission to share mangoes and rasgullas with the jail Superintendent and the staff. The whole experience was almost dream-like, my father told me.

While he was driven back to the convalescent facility, Lady Reid asked Bhushan whether it would be okay if she visited him the following day to, 'follow-up on some additional things I know are on your mind.'

Thinking that he could not have been any luckier, my father said, 'Yes, please. I will wait for you. What time shall I expect you?'

'I would say around 11.30 or so,' replied Lady Reid.

My father had been looking for an anchor. And he had found one in Lady Reid, a woman he had met not too long ago, she had been so kind and generous to him and had extended a hand of support.

My father went straight to his room and simply crashed on his bed. His head was heavy but his heart was light. Until that day, he had not realized how important it was for him to be connected with someone from his family. His elder brother was the first family member he had seen since he left home to join the army—a period during which a lot had happened. My father was happy to see that his brother was in good health and in equally good spirits.

His meeting with Uncle Prabodh also gave him an opportunity to speak with someone about Shingara Singh being on death row and that had made a big difference. Although he had still not been able to find any answers, simply being able to speak about it to someone who he trusted, someone who was a father-figure to him, had helped my father immensely. It was as though a huge burden had been lifted, and perhaps that is why his heart was light and he was feeling better. Another reason that made him feel proud was that for once, it was he and not his brother who had successfully established a connection with someone important, someone who, against all odds, had made the meeting between the brothers possible. Until now, compared to Uncle Prabodh, a 'well-known' personality, my father was someone anonymous.

The chirping of birds outside snapped him out of his reverie, bringing him back to the real world, the convalescent home, the room. Usha would come to visit at around 6.30 p.m., about twenty minutes from now. He knew her routine. She would ask him all sorts of questions, not because she was nosey, but because she was genuinely concerned about him. How much should he hide from Usha, he debated silently.

He was confused; he did not know how much of the truth he owed to Usha. He did not know what measure of truth he owed to Lady Reid. He would have to also decide if he was going to talk about Shingara Singh with Lady Reid. He was almost certain she would ask him questions for which he might not have straight answers; questions that could be about Shingara Singh; questions that only Shingara Singh could answer.

He took a quick cold water bath, a necessity in the hot and humid weather of Calcutta during summer. If one had access to running water, one was well advised to take advantage of it.

Just as expected, at 6.30 p.m. Usha knocked, entered and asked Bhushan about his visit to Alipore Jail. He told her it was an overwhelming experience, since the last time the two brothers had seen each other was before he had left home to join army at barely eighteen years of age. So overtaken by emotion was he that he could barely speak.

Realizing how sensitive the subject was, Usha did not ask him any more questions. After composing himself, Bhushan thanked Usha profusely for having introduced Lady Reid to him. Without Lady Reid, his meeting with Prabodh would not have been possible, he said. Then the conversation moved to things mundane and of mutual interest until it was time for dinner.

Normally my father would be done with dinner by 7.30 p.m., and then he would spend some time with fellow residents. But that evening he decided to head straight back to his room. He wanted to write a thank-you note to Lady Reid. Without wasting any time, he went to his desk and began:

*Respected Lady Reid,*

*I do not even know where to start this. Like most people, I too am shaped by my cultural beliefs. And one of these beliefs is that in life everything happens for a reason. There was a reason that I had to contract cholera and land up at this convalescent facility, so that you could enter my life. You have touched my life with your tender sensitivity.*

*The fact that you enabled two brothers to meet, one on one, in private, speaks of your humanism and your ability to understand the complexity of relationships. I feel that by giving us our privacy, you respected me as an individual and as a human being. For making me feel that way I will forever remain indebted to you.*

*I am not sure what your coming into my life really means. And I do not wish to find meaning in all this. However, I do want to let you know that the kindness and the tenderness you have shown, I will never forget.*

*In the end, I wish there was something I could do for you in return for all that you have done for me.*

*Please accept my respectful regards.*

*Bhushan*

The next day, Lady Reid arrived on her visit as promised. As soon as greetings and pleasantries were exchanged, my father handed her his thank-you note. She read it, seated on the only chair in the room, and then looked at my father and read aloud the last line: 'I wish there was something I could do for you...' Yes, Bhushan, there *is* something you can do for me,' she said, 'Please tell me more about Shingara Singh.'

My father was not ready for this, and this showed in his eyes and his expression.

'Bhushan, look into my eyes,' said Lady Reid, 'You need to trust me. I have come back to see you not because I want to harm you. On the contrary, I have come back because I want to help you.'

My father began, 'Just like me, Shingara Singh is a loyal British soldier, almost my brother's age and was my ardali for over four long years. We went through a lot together, in the action in Burma. He was not only my ardali but also my companion in that journey...' and he broke down.

'What happened?' asked Lady Reid.

My father pulled himself together and said, 'Shingara Singh was investigated in regard to the disappearance of a soldier in my unit. No evidence was ever found against him. I was also questioned but exonerated. Throughout the investigation, Shingara Singh was very cooperative and soldier-like. However, somewhere towards the end of the investigative proceedings, he acted defiantly so as to protect his self-respect, and my honour; an act for which he was charged with attempted murder and was subsequently sentenced to death.' He reached into the scattered pile of old handwritten notes and pulled out a piece of paper that was over one year old, a piece he had written before the disappearance of the soldier from the unit:

> Shingara Singh is a simple villager, an illiterate albeit honest man. Larger issues of life were irrelevant to his day-to-day existence. He knows his limitations, and knows that his service to the cause of India's

independence is as humble as that of a squirrel in constructing the mythical bridge to Lanka. Yet, he remains content. He overturns no trains, sets fire to no buildings, makes no bombs, performs no acts of destruction with indiscriminate enthusiasm, writes no demands or graffiti on walls, and shouts no slogans. Freedom would hardly bring anything for him. His life in free India will not be transformed—neither Gandhiji nor Netaji will ever touch his being. This simple man has only one ambition that deals with his life in the present moment: to serve his Sahib in true military tradition, with devotion and unwavering loyalty. His engagement in life is whittled down to a few questions which I cannot answer with all my education. I feel all the humbler.

In Shingara Singh, I see a new type of hero, simple and elemental, passionate, a true Sikh, a lion. An earthy valiant farmer, who belongs to the martial tradition that today mirrors India's emergence to a new life of self-respect, self-determination and independence.

Bhushan gave the note to Lady Reid.

Lady Reid read the page. She looked at Bhushan and before she could say anything, he murmured, 'This is what I know about Shingara Singh, and this is what I think of him.' After a brief pause, he continued, 'And now this Shingara Singh who I have known during my life in the military, is waiting in some death cell somewhere, I do not know where; he is waiting for his misery to end. Waiting to be hanged! I wish I knew anything more than this.'

Lady Reid held the corner of the desk as though she would fall if she did not. Then she sat down on the chair.

My father walked up to his bed, sat down and holding his head in his hands began sobbing.

Lady Reid filled a glass with water and gave it to him to drink. He had a few sips and somehow managed to contain himself and regain control of his emotions. She drew her chair closer to my father, held his hands and said, 'I know you well enough and I believe in whatever you tell me; I trust you. I like you. You are a decent young man who comes from a good family. You have good ideals. You seem to respect people, and value relationships. While it is true that I am not an Indian, India is my second home. I have lived in your country long enough to feel that I belong here. I may not be able to feel your feelings for Shingara Singh; however, believe me, knowing you, your sensitivities, having read some of your notes, I have a fairly good idea of who you are and what Shingara Singh means to you. Through my social circle, I know people who might be able to help me locate Shingara Singh. If that happens, I can let you know the latest on him. This may be possible only if I can have some particulars on him.'

My father saw a ray of hope in what otherwise seemed to be a hopeless situation and quickly said, 'Let me write it down for you, I carry this information in my heart.' He wrote down all the pertinent details, folded the paper neatly and gave it to Lady Reid.

Taking the paper from him, Lady Reid asked Bhushan if she could read his journal. His mind started racing. Was there anything in his journal that would incriminate Shingara Singh; no, Bhushan was very sure that there was nothing on the subject—not because he was trying to hide anything, but because he had no knowledge about Shingara Singh's role, if any. And above all, he had enough foresight not to document his own views or conjectures that could be incriminating. Having gone through all the possible outcomes that could result from Lady Reid reading his journal, he made up his mind to be totally trusting of her. 'One thing is for sure,' he thought to himself, 'after reading my journal, Lady Reid will probably be the only person who knows so much about me; perhaps even more than I know about myself, and definitely more than anyone else.' And so he decided to hand over his journal to Lady Reid with a request that she would maintain the confidentiality of its contents.

◆

**Note**

*My father was sent to the Army Hospital in Calcutta sometime in July 1945. On 15 August 1945, the US dropped two atomic bombs on Hiroshima and Nagasaki, leading Japan to surrender on 2 September 1945. While the fast pace of global events was to shape the world to come, happenings in my father's life were soon to determine how different pieces of the jigsaw, that was his journey, were to fit together.*

# End of the War, Beginning of the Battle

SOON AFTER the end of the war in the Pacific in September 1945, modalities to grant independence to India started. While the war had ended, my father's battle to find his elusive destination had just begun. But before he could open that battle-front, he wanted to make sure he had done everything he could to learn the fate of Shingara Singh and if possible, to help him in any way he could. He had already taken the first step—he had confided in Lady Reid and had given her the pertinent details about Shingara Singh. This was around the time when Shingara Singh was a prisoner on death row.

Between July and October of 1945, my father's life had

taken him out of his fighting unit into a hospital and then to a convalescent home. This journey had enabled his life to be touched by the tender, loving and magical hands of three women. Kiran was the epitome of the meaning of her name—*ray of light*. For Bhushan, she represented a ray of hope, as she had brought hope into his life; Usha, whose name meant *dawn*, had brought to him the dawn of a new day, a day with new hopes and new promises that things were bound to get better; and finally, there was Lady Reid.

My father did not know what her first name meant. As a matter of fact, he did not even know her first name. He did not know much about her except that she was married to someone important whose last name was Reid. He wondered if her first name had anything to do with what she represented in his life. Maybe she was his mother—the mother he had lost when he was barely five years old. How could that be, Lady Reid was not an Indian. But, then, souls do not belong to one place. They do not belong to one body. He tried to answer his own questions, address his own doubts. She did play the role of a mother—she united two brothers who had not met each other since… since when? He was not sure.

He did not know where or who he belonged to. He felt closer to people he had met in his recent past than to his own family. And it had all started with the complete and unquestioned loyalty of Shingara Singh, his ardali, who had been taken away by the wolves. The ensuing fast pace of events had added three more people to his surrogate family—Kiran, Usha and Lady Reid.

He was afraid that Shingara Singh's fate had been sealed and that he would be laid to rest soon. Or maybe not, he thought sometimes. He lamented he had not even had the chance to say good bye to Shingara Singh. Then he remembered what he had been taught while growing up—never say goodbye, always take leave saying, 'We shall meet again, soon.' But in that situation, under those circumstances, a goodbye would have been perhaps more appropriate. Now that it was time for him to leave Calcutta and go back, where would he go? What would he say to Usha? What should he say to Lady Reid? Should it be goodbye or should it be 'we shall meet again'?

He was not sure. But he was certain that it was time for him to move on. He was a sailboat in a vast ocean. Was the boat adrift, or headed to a destination? He did not know. But he always wondered, and wondered alone. Shingara Singh, Kiran, Usha and now Lady Reid—were all beacons, lighthouses to his sailboat, destined to be his protectors, so that his boat could reach the shore. Safely!

Who could have predicted that he would have ever been able to experience these wonderful, pure, untainted relationships, he thought to himself. Looking back, even he could not believe that he had gone through so much in such a short span of time—and it was not a dream. It was all real.

He started thinking of life in terms of possibilities, possibilities that he could not even imagine; nevertheless, he knew they did exist—he had first-hand experience.

It was October, a week before the beginning of Durga Puja (worship of goddess Durga), the biggest religious festival in Calcutta. Durga Puja was to be followed by the festival of Diwali, the beginning of new year in Indian calendar. He thought of Durga—a calm and serene divine goddess, who had five pair of hands, and rode a tiger. Durga represented shakti or strength, and had the ability to tame a tiger; her hands full of all sorts of weapons that she used to ward off evil forces. Her calm face represented her ability to think and act rationally. Not to be overwhelmed by circumstances, or by any kind of adversity. Goddess Durga is also known as Durga Ma or Mother Durga.

He drew comfort from the fact that somehow his destiny had enabled him to do the best he could to make a difference, *any* difference, in Shingara Singh's situation, in his condition, in his life, whatever of life Shingara Singh was left with. But he wished he could communicate with Shingara Singh just once. The only way he could do that was if he wrote a note to Shingara Singh and leaves it with Lady Reid.

'No, it would be asking for too much. Lady Reid does not even know where Shingara Singh is. Besides, what can I say in a note?' my father thought. He was torn apart; he did not know what to do; he was confused; he could not decide. He did nothing. And that in itself was a decision, although, not out of choice.

Lady Reid's assurance was enough for Bhushan to look forward to the future. He started thinking of Lady Reid: an influential woman—as powerful as she is genteel. Was she Mother Durga? The lady used her position of influence not out of arrogance; but instead to help me unite with my brother. 'Would she be able to ensure divine justice for Shingara Singh?' he asked himself.

Diwali, the Indian New Year, the festival of lights, was only weeks away. It celebrated the return of Lord Rama to his kingdom after an exile of fourteen years; his return to the kingdom where he was born; to a place where he rightfully belonged. My father saw Lord Rama's return as representing his coming of age—he had freed Mother Sita from the clutches of the evil designs of Ravana, someone who was otherwise gifted with a brilliant intellect, his infinite knowledge was depicted through the ten heads he was supposed to have, 'and', thought my father, 'I am returning from a self-imposed exile of almost four years. I fought to free Mother India from the control of wolves. Although millions of lives were lost in the war, in the end goodness prevailed over evil. And I played my role in the history that was in the making. As a victorious soldier, I am going to return home.'

There had been no news from home for a long time. Where is my home, he thought, who is my family? The last he had heard about his family was from someone... who was it? He was unable to recall who it was, but he remembered the information had been passed on to him in the earlier part of the year that Headmaster Satya Dev had been transferred. This forced dislocation was the punishment to the family for Prabodh's adventures against the rulers of the day.

He walked up to the calendar, the only object hanging on the otherwise desolate blank walls of his small room. Diwali was on Saturday, 3 November. He decided that Monday, 5 November would be a good day to leave Calcutta and head west. He did not know his destination. However, he did know that he was going to be homeward bound.

How would he break the news to Usha, what would he tell Lady Reid? He felt so connected to his new family. To feel connected, did one have to be related? No, he didn't think so. Shingara Singh was not related to him, and yet they had formed a strong bond, connected with each other, 'So much so that he sacrificed his life for me, and to protect my honour,' he thought.

He knew that no one expected him to be in Calcutta for an indefinite period of time. He also knew that no one, including himself, expected that the decision to leave Calcutta to go back home would be so fast and so sudden. He felt relieved that 5 November was still a good four weeks away.

# But It Was Not Meant to Be

DURGA PUJA is the one of the biggest festivals in West Bengal. The festivities start about ten days before Diwali, the festival of lights. Small clay lamps called diyas are filled with oil. The lighting of these diyas is meant to dispel darkness and ignorance. It also signifies the light of wisdom. It is also a time when families get together and enjoy themselves. People exchange sweets, temples are crowded with devotees who throng places of worship to atone for their sins. They ask the Goddess for mercy and to forgive the mistakes they may have committed in the past, and pray to Durga to bless them with fortune and good luck for the new year. The celebration is topped with sumptuous feasting.

The year 1945 was no different. Festivities of the season could be felt in the air. For my father, this holiday season was the first that he would be celebrating among civilians, away from home. Yet, it felt to him as if he was going to be with a family—a different kind of family.

Usha had made sure that all residents were invited to join in the events that were to be held on the premises of the convalescent facility. Saturday, 27 October was planned to be the big day of celebrations. Prayers were going to be held later in the morning, followed by a community lunch. An outdoor canopy had been set up, under which everyone would eat together.

Lady Reid was one of the important guests. Although not a Hindu in terms of her religious beliefs, she nevertheless participated in nearly every event to which she was invited. Her active participation in such events enabled her to connect with the community at large, and carried significance for the locals, with whom she had formed a close bond. Durga Puja celebration of 1945 was yet another event where Lady Reid was active with the rest of the participants and devotees.

Prayers and worship were over by noon. For lunch, everyone gathered under the canopy and sat down on the floor to eat. Since my father was not from Bengal, the whole event was a first-time experience for him. During his time in the army, he had never seen British officers mingling with Indian soldiers so freely. There, hierarchy of status and relationships was obvious at every get together. Here, he not only saw Lady Reid mingling freely with the locals, but also witnessed her participating in religious rituals with the same enthusiasm that he witnessed in the locals.

Lady Reid asked my father and Usha to sit next to her for lunch. Everyone enjoyed the simple food. After the meal was over, Lady Reid asked my father if she could speak to him about something important. My father suggested they could meet in his room, since he had no other place he could call his own. And so they walked to his room, my father anxious and a bit apprehensive since he had no idea what Lady Reid wanted to talk about. They entered the room, and he offered Lady Reid a chair and sat on the edge of his bed.

Lady Reid informed my father that she had forwarded the particulars of Shingara Singh to appropriate individuals, with a request that his case be reviewed thoroughly and with compassion. This review would be in addition to the appeal process that Shingara Singh was entitled to. Lady Reid also informed him that she had reason to believe that Shingara Singh's case would be looked into with sympathy and compassion. And before my father could say anything, Lady Reid asked him, 'Diwali is fast approaching, what are your plans for it?'

'I am going to request an honourable discharge from the army and head back west, to Lahore,' replied my father.

'But I thought you came from Multan,' said Lady Reid.

'That is correct. That is where my home was when I joined the army. But I understand that since then my father has been transferred to Lahore, about 150 miles north-east of Multan. And that is where I am going to go soon after Diwali.'

Lady Reid unbuttoned the shoulder bag she was carrying and took out my father's journal. 'It has been an experience to read your writings, Bhushan,' she said. 'Reading this journal has enabled me to understand who you are, what your beliefs are, and what you stand for. I want to make a request to you.'

'You are elder to me; you do not have to make a request; please simply ask me what I can do for you. You have done so much for me,' replied my father. 'It will be my honour to do anything for you. Although, I do not know if I will be able to deliver what you ask for, I will do my best.'

'I do not know how to say it in any other way than to be straight and direct. I wonder, Bhushan, if you would be willing to come with me to England as my adopted son!'

My father had not expected this at all. The request came as a total surprise to him; something that he would not have expected even in his wildest dreams. 'As it is, I already feel so indebted to you for all that you have done for me,' he said. 'You reconnected me with my elder brother. You have already done so much to help me with Shingara Singh's situation. I do not know if I would ever be able to reciprocate all your favours. Now I am overwhelmed, I do not know how to respond to you,' he said simply.

'I know nobody is waiting for me to return home. I do not even know if I am going to go back home, or if I am simply going and visiting a place I think is my home. However, I do know that I belong to this soil. I belong to the people who live in my country. I belong to these bustling crowded streets. Going with you would mean saying goodbye to everything that I can identify with,' he said. 'I hope that you do not take my saying all this as if I do not value what you have just offered. However, it is important for me to be as honest with you as I can be with myself.'

◆

My father spent the next few days completing the formalities for his discharge from the army. He also made sure that he spent as much time as was possible with all the people he had befriended.

His belongings included one little suitcase, a shoulder bag that contained his valuable companions—his journal, three separate stacks of papers neatly put together in one little leather binder. The first stack of papers was blank, while the second stack had my father's hand-written notes. And the third one had typed pages, some of them with dates, while others were without any reference to time. The leather binder that held all this, had been his companion through the turbulent years in the army. Although it looked used up, in reality after years of use, it had some patches that had acquired a darker hue and were both soft and smooth to touch. They gave the flap of the bag its distinctive character. These patches gave away its age—just as the wrinkles on the face of an elderly man are a good indicator of what the man has experienced in his life. The leather binder was neatly tied with a string.

However, the two most important possessions he was carrying with him could not be seen—the promise from Lady Reid to do everything she could to help Shingara Singh, and the wonderful memories of his new-found family. This new family of relationships started with Shingara Singh, in quick succession had added Usha, Kiran and Lady Reid to its fold. This was his new family, away from the family he had been born into. And now he was to leave all this behind—in search of a new destination, a sailboat headed to a new port of call.

My father left Calcutta on his way to Lahore, a journey that would have taken him five days to complete by train. Delhi was the main hub for transit trains. Once he reached Delhi, he decided to take a little diversion. Instead of going straight to Lahore, he decided to visit a couple of childhood friends pursuing higher education in a city called Hoshiarpur, about 100 miles east of his final destination, Lahore.

Hoshiarpur is a city in the foothills of lower Himalayan mountain ranges (in a range called the Shivalik Hills), the area was known for its delicious mangoes at the time, considered one of best in Punjab, east of river Ravi. In addition to mangoes, Hoshiarpur was also known for one of the best institutions of higher learning—University College of Hoshiarpur. This is where two of my father's childhood friends were attending college in pursuit of education. University College, Hoshiarpur, was known for its liberal arts programme—especially Economics and Political Science.

During his three-day and two-night visit, my father was exposed to one of the best educational institutions in the region. Far from the war zone, the place was bustling with the life and energy of young students, who were full of hope and enthusiasm. This energy could be felt all around. These young men were there for a specific purpose—to prepare themselves to take charge of their own destiny and the destiny of the new independent India that was sure to be born but no one knew exactly when. Some of the graduates from this era would include noted civil servants and bureaucrats, such as Prof. R.C. Paul, who would later become Vice Chancellor, Punjab University, Chandigarh, and Dr Manmohan Singh, an economist and bureaucrat who would go on to become the fourteenth Prime Minister of India, holding office for two terms, and the first Sikh to hold that post.

This environment was totally different and absolutely new for my father. Young men, fully charged with the spirit to free India from the clutches of the British and transform her from a colony to an independent country, could be seen all around. The last four years of his life had been full of death, destruction and precariousness. In contrast, he noticed that life as a college student was not only much easier but also very meaningful, allowing the mind to be creative. All that one needed to do was to devote time to books and stay focused. It did not take him too long to make a pledge to himself that he was going to finish college and earn his Masters in Political Science.

He spent the next year-and-a-half in Lahore, where he acclimatized himself to civilian life and did odd jobs. He enrolled in the Faculty of Arts programme at Foreman Christian (FC) College, Lahore. It was and continues to be a very reputed educational institution, and it prepared him well to attend University College, Hoshiarpur.

India became independent in August, 1947. The blessed birth of a new independent India came with the slashing of her heart to make way for a new country: Pakistan—the land of the pure—that is what Pakistan literally means. As a result of this partition, more than ten million people were uprooted from their homeland on both sides of the border, and were forced to flee on foot, by bullock carts and trains. They were all refugees, abandoned souls in search of a place they could call home. And among those refugees was twenty-three year old Bhushan and his entire family. They all had to flee Lahore, a city that was now within the boundaries of Pakistan. Overnight, the partition made both countries a forbidden place to millions of people who were forced to cross to the other side.

My father was one of the passengers on that infamous train, which, in addition to carrying the lucky ones, also carried the mutilated dead bodies of people who had been killed, both Halaal and Jhatka. He was one of the lucky ones on that train. His cart was guarded by fearless defendants of their own faith, their own dignity: the Nihangs; well-acknowledged fighters among Sikhs. However, his luck did not protect him from seeing people being beheaded like animals. Under those horrible conditions, somehow, he safely made it to Hoshiarpur.

My father had a very good academic record that included an associate degree from FC College, Lahore. This was further supplemented by his service in the British Army. However, in spite of these credentials, he had to fight to get into a degree programme at University College, Hoshiarpur.

Every applicant for admission to this institution, had to take a written pledge that while they were a student in that institution, they would not join any political party and would not participate in any strikes or public protests—something that was a natural outcome of newly won freedom: college students would find any excuse to start a protest and a call for strike. To keep educational institutions politically neutral, students indulging in disruptive activities would be expelled from school. However, for my father, to sign such a pledge was not only unacceptable but also went against the very core of independence—something he had actively fought for. He refused to sign the pledge and that refusal resulted in a student strike. Eventually, Prof. Vishwanath, the then Vice Chancellor intervened, my father was admitted to the University, and the strike was called off.

He completed his Master's Degree in Political Science and also finished some graduate work in English literature. By the mid-1950s, he had completed his education and made Hoshiarpur his base at least for the time being. He started a tutoring academy for college students, where he taught English and Political Science. This arrangement gave him plenty of time to spare that he would use writing stories for Urdu newspapers.

By the early 1960s, he had married and moved to New Delhi where he was working as a Senior Research Officer in the Ministry of Information & Broadcasting. His wife, my mother Pushpa, who came from a family of teachers, was Vice-Principal of a High School not too far from where the family lived in a posh area of South Delhi. The family—my parents and the three of us children—lived in a two-bedroom flat with modern amenities. It was by any standards, a significant achievement for someone who had come as a refugee from Pakistan just thirteen years earlier with almost nothing to call his own.

Uncle Prabodh had done well too and was already a part of the ruling establishment of India. He had known Nehru from the days of the freedom struggle, and Nehru was now India's first Prime Minister. So close was his association with Nehru that as his private and secret emissary, Uncle Prabodh had conducted behind the scenes negotiations with Sheikh Abdullah, and in March 1948, barely six months after India's independence, had arranged for Sheikh Abdullah to return from Pakistan to India and take charge as the first Prime Minister of the State of Kashmir. Uncle Prabodh's political base was in the State of Punjab, while his family lived in New Delhi.

# The Hidden Hand of Destiny

Uncle Prabodh had four children—two sons Pawan and Ashwani, whom the family affectionately called Pammi and Ammu respectively, and two daughters Priya, affectionately called Munna, and Aashi. Pammi was a handsome, mild mannered, affectionate and down-to-earth young man. He was close to his Uncle Bhushan. I remember vividly as four-year old, Pammi visiting our small house in a chauffeur-driven car. Sometimes, for reasons of privacy, he would sneak out of his mansion on a scooter and call home only to let someone in the house know that he was at his father's younger brother's house.

Uncle Prabodh had planned that his son Pawan would run a factory in Batala—a town on the Indian border with

Pakistan. It would be a launching pad, the means for the young man to start building his political base and establish himself as the representative of the people from that part of Punjab. Batala was part of Uncle Prabodh's parliamentary constituency that he had nurtured and represented since the 1950s. A budding industrial town, it was known as the Manchester of Punjab, because of the many small foundries and factories that made lathe and milling machines, and all kinds of agricultural implements that were partly responsible for the Green Revolution[2] in Punjab.

Uncle Prabodh, through his close association with the ruling elite in the state capital as well as Delhi, the capital of India 300 miles south-east of Batala, was able to get significant amount of federal money to fund the growth of these small scale industrial enterprises. In the process, he had generated a lot of goodwill and there were a lot of people who would be indebted to him forever, since they were the beneficiaries of all the good things he had done for the state of Punjab and especially for this small border town.

He was the guest of honour for events at local schools and the only college in town, where he would generously give out grants for the improvement of buildings or to pay for books

---

[2] Refers to a period in the late 1960s and the 1970s when high-yielding varieties of crop were introduced in Punjab and resulted in high-growth, dubbed the Green Revolution.

and tuition of students who were too poor to afford the luxury of an education. He was a man of masses, who truly believed that education is the key to bring a family out of poverty and assure the overall improvement of living conditions. Therefore, he strongly advocated spread of education especially in rural areas of the state of Punjab. As the Speaker of the House of State Legislatures, and as the Minister of Education for the state, he allocated special funds for primary and middle schools in rural areas and for the hiring of women teachers. This in turn would help increase the enrolment of girls in primary schools. In addition to having populist ideas, he was a visionary, able to think way beyond his time.

Back in New Delhi, one day when Pawan visited his Uncle Bhushan, he was not too happy to share with him that within a few days he would be going to Punjab for an extended period of time. There he would be introduced to his father's associates. My father counselled him telling him that if nothing else, he would get to meet the people his father represented.

'But Chachaji,' said Pawan, 'that does not interest me. Besides, if that is how I wanted to spend my life—meeting influential people—I should be looking for individuals who are more influential than my own father, not people who look up to him for small favours.' Nevertheless, Pawan went to Chandigarh, the capital of Punjab, which would be his base and where Uncle Prabodh spent much of his time conducting the affairs of the state in various capacities that included Speaker of the House, Minister of Education and a member of the State Legislature.

A few days later my father got a message from Uncle Prabodh asking him to reach Chandigarh immediately, because Pawan was very sick and had been admitted to the local state of the art hospital in Chandigarh. There was shock and gloom in the family and my father rushed from Delhi to Chandigarh. In those days it took about six to seven hours by car. By the time he reached, Uncle Prabodh had arranged for a doctor to be flown in from England. It was a case of a ruptured appendix and Pawan's blood had been infected.

My father was at his bedside, and so was Uncle Prabodh. Pawan knew he was not going to make it and with one hand holding my father's hand and with the other his father's hand, tears flowing down his face he asked my father to promise him he would start the factory in Batala. Those were his last words. But he was able to hear his uncle Bhushan's silence acquiescing to his wish.

After the last rites were over, and things had settled down, Uncle Prabodh came to see my father in his small two-bedroom flat in New Delhi. This was unusual, Uncle Prabodh was not only an influential and important person, but also much older than my father. Under such circumstances, it was the younger brother who was supposed to visit the elder. Nevertheless, it was my uncle who came down to visit his younger brother and tearfully requested him and his wife to move to Batala to fulfil Pawan's last wish—to start the factory in Batala. This was something Pushpa, my mother, was absolutely against. She had her own reasons—both her brothers were very well-established in New Delhi. Two of her four sisters lived within six miles of where our family lived. My mother had her whole career ahead of her. And so she did not want to leave New Delhi and move to a small, dusty town, 300 miles away from Delhi, the capital of India and a city where she had always felt at home.

In the family tradition that my father grew up in, an elder brother was a father figure. However, in this particular case due to Uncle Prabodh's position and his status, it would have been even more difficult for my father to decline any request of his. And as if this were not enough, the overwhelmingly tragic circumstances under which the promise had been made to a dying nephew made it almost impossible for my father to deny the wish. He was bound to honour it.

Therefore, overlooking his wife's considerations, during the summer of 1963 my father decided to move the family to Batala. This would prove to be perhaps one of the most significant decisions he made in his married life, as far as I know. A decision he would regret later, on the one hand, and would accept as fate on the other. The move to Batala was perhaps one such event.

My father vaguely recalled that Shingara Singh came

from a village called Ghasitpura, a hamlet of perhaps 30 to 40 families, not too far from Batala. The village was just off the main road that connected Amritsar with the state of Jammu & Kashmir about 300 miles further north. He remembered Shingara Singh telling him that his native village was less than five miles away from Batala.

Although my father had played a pivotal role in getting Shingara Singh's death sentence commuted through the help he received from Lady Reid and his older brother Prabodh, he and Shingara Singh had never had an opportunity to meet since the episode when a British officer had grilled my father and Shingara Singh about the latter's role in the disappearance of a soldier who had misbehaved with my father. That final meeting had culminated with the British officer yelling at Bhushan, 'You Indian bastards, you always protect your own, don't you?', and Shingara Singh had shouted back at the officer in Gurumukhi, his native language, 'You firangies, may not understand our language but we understand yours. This is not how you are supposed to talk to my Sahib, your fellow officer!' With his right hand on his kirpan, he had lurched towards the British officer, shouting, '*Jo Bole So Nihal… Sat Sri Akal.*'

My father had never forgotten that final courageous act of defiance by Shingara Singh in defence of his 'Sahib'. That kirpan represented a tradition of courage and honour, passed down by Sikh Gurus, notably the last Guru, Guru Gobind Singh, who had fought twenty battles against the Mughals from the late 1670s to 1708 in defence of the motherland.

The Guru's story had taught Shingara Singh to fight against injustice, to stand up and fight against any kind of oppression anytime and anywhere, regardless of consequences. And so Shingara Singh's response to the British officer's insult, was to leap to protect and defend his Sahib's honour and respect. More than two-hundred years after the passing of the tenth Guru, Shingara Singh had taken a stand against the invaders of his generation, as manifested in the British officer.

My father was often haunted by the look in Shingara Singh's eyes as he was being dragged out of that room, to an unknown fate. He was looking at my father as if to say, 'Please forgive me, Sahib, for having put you through all this…'

My father was not sure if fifteen years of India's independence would have changed anything in Shingara Singh's life, his family, or his village. He also wondered if Shingara Singh had anything to do with the disappearance of that missing soldier. And if he did have any role, what was it, and why? My father could only speculate. Truth was a receding horizon.

One day, sometime in the winter of 1963–64, my father decided to look for Shingara Singh. He borrowed a car from one of his friends to visit Ghasitpura. Batala, population 80,000, had only three families that owned a car. The country, in the 1960s, was passing through the bicycle age.

It was late in the afternoon. After a twenty-minute

drive, he reached Ghasitpura and started making enquiries about Shingara Singh, the only name he knew in the family. Nobody seemed to have heard the name. Disappointed at not being able to locate Shingara Singh and about to leave, he was stopped by an elderly member of the village council, the Panchayat. He joined the few villagers who had gathered around my father. The elderly man asked him if he could be of any help. My father explained that he was looking for Shingara Singh, who once served in the army.

'The one who also fought in the war?' the man asked.

'Yes. Yes! He is the one I am looking for,' replied my father excitedly, although he had no idea if this elderly man was talking about the same Shingara Singh. It was the answer of a desperate man bent upon pursuing every possible lead to find a lost person. Besides, what were the odds that a small village would have more than one Shingara Singh, and even if it did that the other Shingara Singh or Singhs had also served in the army in World War II.

'It has been years since Shingara Singh passed away, Sahib.'

The words hit my father like a bullet. His mind was able to play out his entire association of over four years with Shingara Singh in less than three seconds. Left speechless, he quietly began walking to his car to leave.

'Sahib,' said the elderly man, 'You have come all the way looking for Shingara Singh. I do not know where you have come from, but since you are here, so close to where Shingara

Singh once lived, at least take a moment to see his family, they live not too far from here.'

This was an idea that had not even passed through my father's mind.

In that world during 1960s, the word *family* had a meaning that was inclusive: it included your wife and children, of course. But it also included your brothers, sisters, their spouses, your nieces and nephews, and even the grandchildren of your siblings, constituting a wide network of close kinships.

The elderly man led my father down a dirt path. After a few minutes of walking through the fields, he was guided to a mud dwelling. Stray dogs were going about their routine. Calling this dwelling a house would be a misnomer. There were a few chickens running around. My father's guide, the elderly member of the village council approached a man with a long beard, sunken eyes and sunken cheeks, dressed in a loose turban and a long, tethered kurta down to his knees. Barefoot, with his hands folded, this man looked much older than his age. He bowed and asked my father how he could be of help. The village elder turned to my father and said, 'Sahib, he is Bahadur Singh, Shingara Singh's younger brother.' Greetings were exchanged.

My father looked at the village elder. Sometimes your eyes do the talking for you. You do not need to say anything, even if you are meeting someone for the first time. It was perhaps one of those looks that he gave to the man. Or perhaps it was just something about the village elder, which drew such a simple, wordless communication from my father? Perhaps my father sensed that the village elder was intuitive enough to have a good feel of people around him. After all, he was trustworthy enough for the residents of the village to come to him to have their minor disputes resolved and arguments settled. They trusted him and his judgment. He was the wise old man. The presence of such elders in the community, who had earned so much trust and respect, made many otherwise complex matters in life very simple.

As a member of the village council, the Panchayat, he did not need to know the law. For a fair and quick resolution of any dispute, he needed to know only two things: what was the truth; and what was right. The residents of the village had agreed that his word would be final, since he was the village elder—a wise man.

Now the village elder looked back at my father and with hands folded, bowed and finally introduced himself, 'I am Balwant. Balwant Singh. People here call me Bapu. I have lived my whole life here, in this village. And I knew Shingara Singh well, very well. If you are his Sahib, he waited for you. He knew one day you would come. For now, I will take your leave. However, I expect I will be seeing you later.' And the village elder exchanged a few words with Bahadur Singh and walked slowly away, leaving my father alone with Bahadur Singh.

Bahadur Singh led him into a mud-walled room with a thatched roof. In the room was a young calf from a cow that the family owned. This calf could not have been more than a day old. There was a cot in one corner, falling apart. Bahadur Singh offered the cot to my father while he himself sat on the dirt floor, near his feet. My father told Bahadur Singh who he was and that Shingara Singh had served with him in the British Army. He was not sure if, or how much, Bahadur Singh knew of Shingara Singh's association with him. He did not know if Bahadur Singh was aware of what he and Shingara Singh had endured together.

He learned that Shingara Singh had passed away a few months after he returned to his village in early 1948. That winter of 1948 had been bitter and cut like a knife. Shingara Singh fell ill. He began spitting up blood and soon it was evident that he had tuberculosis. His family did not have money for the treatment he badly needed. Since it was soon after the partition of India in August 1947, everything was in chaos. Shingara Singh and his family were on 'this side' of the border, an artificial line that divided the two countries. Since they were on 'this side' they did not have to migrate. However, this artificial boundary line was real for people whose lives were changed forever.

My father recalled what he himself had endured during the 1947 partition. It was the largest forced migration of human beings, a result of the decision taken by politicians who were trusted by all. The partition led to the migration of more than ten million people, including my father's entire family. He could only imagine what Shingara Singh and his family must have endured, living in a village so close to the border.

If it was a village that did not have a doctor in 1960s, it certainly could not have had one in 1947–48. My father also concluded that more than likely Shingara Singh had contracted the disease while he was in jail, on death row, waiting to be 'hanged till he is dead', for his act of defiance to protect his Sahib's honour. He remembered Shingara Singh's simple questions. He remembered the dreams Shingara Singh had shared with him; dreams of what freedom would bring to him, to his family, and to his village.

The rewards brought by fifteen years of freedom to the family of a 'freedom fighter' were all too evident to my father—what Shingara Singh himself experienced of free India were only two things, the first that he died a free man, and the second that he died in his village, with his family, among his own and not as an 'unknown soldier'.

My father sat down next to Bahadur Singh, on the skeleton of the cot in the corner of the room, held his hands and asked him what Shingara Singh had shared with the family about his experiences of working in the army and being a world away from home for so many years.

'He always talked about you, Sahib,' said Bahadur Singh,

'he was proud to have served under you. He told us that you never treated him like an ardali, that you were very different from all other officers he had served. He told us that you were very fond of writing and he wished he could write like you. He even started to learn to write in Gurumukhi, a language he could barely read. He knew that one day you would come looking for him. He was very sad that he was not going to be around to see you. He wanted to tell you something in person. He knew that he did not have enough time left for that to happen. None of us in the family know how to write. So, he ended up asking Bapu to write for him.'

'What did he want to tell me?' my father asked.

'I do not know, Sahib. He was alone with Bapu. However, you will find it is all written in there, Sahib.'

'What is written where?'

'Sahib, I do not know how to read. Besides, it is sealed. The only thing I know is that the envelope outside says that it needs to be opened by you only. When Bapu handed me the envelope in Shingara Singh's presence, Shingara told me to always keep it in a safe place. Although a poor man's house is always safe because there is nothing to steal, yet to be sure, I have saved it right there in that suitcase.'

Bahadur Singh got up, opened the suitcase, digging deep all the way down and pulled out an old brown envelope. 'I cannot even tell you, Sahib, how many times I wondered if you would ever come. But at the same time I also thought of my dying brother. The last two days of his life were very painful for him, Sahib. To numb his pain, we gave him a lot of rum. He was going in and out. Every time he realized where he was, he would ask me if I had kept the envelope at a safe place. I was by his side. I had given him my word, a promise given to a dying man that I would save this envelope and wait for you to come. I had no choice but to respect my brother's belief. Belief, that one day you will come looking for him. And here you are!'

And my father thought of the promise he had made to his dying nephew, Pawan. It was one of the outcomes of his keeping the promise that he was there in Shingara Singh's village, the village of Shingara Singh's dreams.

'This is it, Sahib. This is what he wanted to tell you. It is all written in here. You can read it.' Walking slowly towards him, Bahadur Singh gave the envelope to my father, who held it gently and examined both sides of the envelope. The front of the envelope read in English: 'For My Sahib'. From the handwriting it would be obvious to anyone that the writer was learning how to write English.

He opened the envelope. There was only a one-page note, written in Punjabi and signed at the end in English: 'Shingara Singh'.

Shingara Singh had remembered that his Sahib spoke Punjabi but did not know how to read or write the language. And perhaps that is why Shingara Singh wrote on the outside

'For My Sahib', in English and then again, inside he had signed his name in English.

Shingara Singh had kept his promise that one day he would tell his story—a story that all of a sudden was my father Bhushan's most valued possession. He hoped he would find the answer to the question that had haunted him all these years.

Shingara Singh had done the best he could to make sure that my father knew who the envelope was from. My father sought Bahadur Singh's permission to keep the envelope at least for a few days. He was not sure who he was going to request to read the letter to him. The first and the only person who came to his mind was Balwant Singh. This was because the only way my father could keep Shingara Singh's honour was by maintaining the confidentiality of the contents of the letter, contents that were not known even to Bahadur Singh. Contents that were known only to Bapu, who had known them since the day the letter was dictated to him.

And when was that, my father wondered.

He was keen to know the contents of the note, but there was only so much he could take in one afternoon. He decided that the contents would have to reveal themselves some other day. Meanwhile, what was very evident was that Bahadur Singh's family lived in misery. Of the little land the family had initially owned, they were left only with a couple of acres. The rest had been either grabbed by the local landlord or had been mortgaged or leased out because there had been no other option. The family owned a few heads of cattle. The only area where the family had progressed was its own size.

Bahadur Singh had promised his dying elder brother that he would take care of his unfulfilled responsibilities, i.e. taking care of the family. In accordance with the local custom of the day and with the approval of the village elders, the unmarried Bahadur Singh ended up marrying his sister-in-law, Shingara Singh's widow and fathered four children with her, in addition to the three children she had borne to Shingara Singh.

The eldest child she bore from Bahadur Singh was their son Jarnail Singh and everyone called him Jaila. The second child, another son, was Parru—his name meant someone who was going to learn how to read and write, someone who was going to be a learned and wise man. As opposed to Jarnail Singh, Parru did attend high school. And the third child was a daughter whose name I did not learn until much later. Apart from these three was Karnail Singh, the eldest son the family had from Shingara Singh, in addition to the two daughters Shingara Singh had fathered. The daughters were married off by the time we got to know the family and therefore, I never got to know them well.

That day my father wanted to do something for the family. Maybe it was a repayment for the fierce loyalty of Shingara Singh—loyalty my father never demanded, loyalty he never got an opportunity to openly acknowledge, loyalty for which he never got to say a simple 'thank you'.

'Why didn't I try to locate Shingara Singh earlier?' he asked himself. 'Why did I let time just slip by? Why did I let life just slip by?' He felt emotionally drained and wished he could turn back the wheel of time. That was not possible. He could not even stop time. He knew he could not.

He held Bahadur Singh by the shoulders and said, 'It has taken me all these years to reconnect with you and the family of my dear friend Shingara Singh. My destiny has brought me back to a place I had only heard of. It has brought me to a family that I feel I have known since I met Shingara Singh more than twenty years ago. Now you do not have to struggle alone. Now I am going to help you keep the word you gave to my dying friend, your elder brother Shingara Singh. I am here with you to share those responsibilities. From now on, things are going to change for you, for me, and for all of us.' And although Bahadur Singh did not know what my father really meant, but he could feel the warmth, passion and honesty behind what he had just heard.

My father walked out of the mud-walled room, followed by Bahadur Singh. Other members of the family were outside. They included a woman, waiting with a glass of water. She had her head and face covered with a worn-out but very colourful long thin cotton veil.

'She is my wife, Sahib,' said Bahadur Singh. Turning towards his wife he said, 'Shingara Singh was Sahib's ardali during the war. And he is the same Sahib who made Shingara Singh's release from the jail possible.'

My father could not see her face. He did not really need to. He needed only her presence; the presence that gave him an instant opportunity to do something for the family. He took some money out from the inside breast pocket of his jacket, and gave it as a gift to Shingara Singh's widow, now Bahadur Singh's wife because he was seeing her for the first time.

Was he giving the gift-blessing to Shingara Singh's wife, his widow? Then he reminded himself that she was not a widow anymore. She was married and she was his new friend Bahadur Singh's wife, mother of his children, mother of Shingara Singh's children.

The woman touched my father's feet, seeking his blessings. And Bahadur Singh followed her. My father gave Bahadur Singh a firm hug, and asked him to visit him.

The driver who had brought my father to the village, was sitting in the car enjoying the afternoon sun, totally oblivious to the happenings of the last hour. As soon as my father entered the car, he started the engine and the car left the village to go back to Batala. As he was being driven to Batala, my father saw the sun coming down, marking end of another day.

But what a day! He had discovered that a significant part of his past was only five miles away from his present place of residence. And he had found out where Shingara Singh came from. What those unfulfilled dreams of an independent India would have meant to Shingara Singh, he wondered.

My father had yet to find out what Shingara Singh had requested to be written in that note. The note that was in that envelope and the envelope was there, right next to him. Bhushan touched and felt the envelope. He wished the envelope could speak.

At one level he was afraid; afraid of what the note might tell him. He knew whatever was in the note, it certainly was going to be the truth. 'Essentially,' he silently told himself, 'I am afraid of finding out the truth.' He looked at the envelope. His eyes blurred. The envelope was staring at him with Shingara Singh's name on it—the name that Shingara Singh had learned to write, that too in English.

As they drove, he spotted a roadside eatery, a dhaba, essentially a truck-stop for long-haul truck drivers. He asked his driver to pull over. He got enough food packed for about twenty adults. From the local liquor shop, he also bought the most expensive bottle of liquor and headed back to Bahadur Singh's village.

That sunny afternoon of a mild winter day marked the beginning of a new relationship between Bhushan and Shingara Singh's, now Bahadur Singh's family. As a follow-up to the assurance he had given Bahadur Singh that 'things were not going to be the same for him and his family', the first thing he did was to employ Bahadur Singh in the factory that Bhushan was just setting up—the factory in the name of a silent promise given to his nephew Pawan, Uncle Prabodh's elder son, minutes before Pawan's tragic death following a ruptured appendix.

I have clear memories of Bahadur Singh working in our factory. And the only way I can describe Bahadur Singh's job is that of an 'unskilled' labourer. I vividly recall Bahadur Singh using a shovel to load the basket with dirt in one corner and carrying it on his head to the other corner of the factory. As a young boy, sometimes, I would count how many times Bahadur Singh performed the same task. I would calculate how much dirt he moved in one day. Perhaps, it was also my way of feeling proud, I could create my own simple math riddles and solve them without anyone's help. To this day, I cannot figure out why Bahadur Singh would not use a wheelbarrow.

I also remember that Bahadur Singh would walk from Ghasitpura to our factory every day and then walk back, about a ten-mile round trip. He did not know how to ride a bicycle and could not afford any other means of transport. Many workers in the factory used to resent Bahadur Singh because they thought he was a lazy man who did not work hard enough. Little did anyone know the special relationship my father had with Bahadur Singh.

Perhaps it was due to this special relationship that I recall that Bahadur Singh was the only worker in the factory (among over fifty employees), who could and who would walk up to our house to see us, or even have a word with my mother. I remember Bahadur Singh would sometimes come up to our house, just to check on us and my mother to see how we all were doing. He well understood the adjustment the family was going through, having moved from a big city to a small town. He would ask my mother if there was anything he or his family could do to make our life more comfortable in our new home.

I have fond memories of those rare occasions when Bahadur Singh would come to see my mother. She would always cover her head out of respect for someone who was older than her husband, just as she did when she would be in front of my grandfather, or even Uncle Prabodh. This was just one dimension of her relationship with Bahadur Singh, respecting him like an elder member of the family. The other dimension was her frustration with their generosity. This would manifest in the plentiful supply of fresh milk every day, and fresh jaggery made the previous night from fresh sugarcane juice. For a husband and wife with three young children, these daily gifts were a headache in terms of how much the family could consume.

I remember once my mother very tactfully and unsuccessfully, requested Bahadur Singh to slow down on the supply of milk saying, 'Could you please ask Bibi not to give us so much milk since it is getting spoiled.' The supply of milk was cut down, only to be substituted by clarified butter as we would call it, desi ghee. It could be stored for a long time without getting spoiled. And no refrigeration required!

By now, Bahadur Singh's son Jarnail Singh, who had dropped out in fifth grade, was a young teenager. He dropped out because as a strong and responsible young boy of the family, it was his duty to spend his time and effort in supporting the family, not wasting his time in useless home assignments from his school teacher. After all, time spent on those assignments was not going to bring the cows home or get them their fresh feed. Time spent working in the fields, or working in our house doing mundane chores was going to bring extra money to the cash-strapped family. One of the tasks Jaila would perform around our house was to iron our clothes, something he became very good at within a few weeks.

Almost thirty-five years later, while my father was still alive, I asked him why he had Jaila work in our house. Why did he not insist that Bahadur Singh send Jaila to school? My father told me that sending Jaila to a school in the village would have been a luxury for the family, a luxury that the family could not afford. He was a precious resource to be used in the little farm land the family still had in the village. Nor would Bahadur Singh accept any more than my father was already giving, by way of monetary help. He had pride and self-respect and wanted to pay back my father for all that he was doing for him and his family

I remember one summer Jaila became an obvious choice of replacement for Loakmani, our home help, who had moved from Delhi to Batala with us. Loakmani had gone back to his village in the mountainous Garhwal region. Once every three to four years he would visit his family in a village in the foothills. That particular summer, the summer of 1967, gave me an opportunity to spend more time with Jaila than I would have otherwise. During this summer, Jaila taught me how to ride a bicycle. I remember while I would ride my bicycle, Jaila would run with me assuring me every step of the way that he would not let me fall.

During the winter months, our family would hire a horse carriage called tonga, for the day and go over to Ghasitpura and spend the entire day there, in the village. The Bahadur Singh family would be making jaggery from the fresh sugarcane juice and would give us jaggery mixed with roasted peanuts. In the West, this rustic candy would be known as Peanut Brittle.

Bahadur Singh's wife, we affectionately called her Bibi, would cook saag (a dish made with mustard leaves), and makki ki roti (cornbread tortilla) for us. From material standards, the family had little to offer. Yet they had the most precious thing in abundance—love and affection combined with generous hospitality and that too unconditional, without expecting anything in return.

After my mother's untimely demise in July 1969, our relationship with the Bahadur Singh family continued. They would supply us fresh milk every day. By the time I was in eighth grade, I would go to the village on my bicycle, spend the day with the family, playing with the oxen who would work the whole day pulling water out from a well with the help of that hoary mechanical device, the persian wheel. Memories of many visits to the Bahadur Singh family in Ghasitpura are fresh in my mind—as though all this had happened just yesterday.

It was during one of those visits, when Bahadur Singh asked me to take a walk with him over to the fields where male members of his family were busy at work. As we were walking together, I asked Bahadur Singh how come he did not have a tractor, something, as a child I associated with farming. And for me, Bahadur Singh was a farmer. Although, at that moment, the question was more of a wish, since I knew, if Bahadur Singh did have one, I would be able to at least get a ride while it was being used in the fields, and perhaps even hold the steering wheel, pretending to be a tractor driver and a farmer at the same time!

'Well,' he answered, 'First of all, you have to have money to pay for a tractor. And second, you have to have a farm big enough that you can really justify the need for a tractor. We do not have enough money to buy one and we do not have enough land to justify one.'

Now that forty years later I have come to know a few things about Shingara Singh, I can see the similarities between the simple questions Shingara Singh would ask my father, and the simple answers Bahadur Singh gave me during those walks through the fields.

Thanks to the help they got from my father, slowly but surely things started to change for Bahadur Singh's family. Perhaps the turning point came in the mid-1970s when my father helped the family get a big chunk of their land back from a long-term lease the family had signed with a local brick-kiln owner. My father had enough influence and clout in the small town by now to get things done—all he needed to do was to make a phone call to the right person.

By this time, Bahadur Singh's family had enough livestock to supply milk to many restaurants and families in Batala. And one family that they always took special care of was ours. In 1977, I left Batala in pursuit of higher education, first for Amritsar, and then for Chandigarh, and finally, in 1984 for the US. Although my contact with the family pretty much ended in 1977, they always stayed in my mind. I never forgot their unwavering loyalty and gratitude, particularly for my father.

The next ten years—1984 to 1994—I spent finishing my MBA and establishing myself in the US, and finally settling down and getting married.

*A Punjab Defence Post at the Battle of Kohima*

*The War Memorial in Kohima.
In April 1944, the Japanese invasion of
India was put to a halt at Kohima.*

*Dev Brat Varma, affectionately called Bhushan, c.1955*

*Bahadur Singh (aged 92), 2008*

*Bhushan, c.1992*

*Retired Headmaster Satya Dev at the age of 97*

*The moment of reconnect:*
*Rajesh with Bahadur Singh, December 2008*

*Rajesh with Bahadur Singh, 1996*

*Bahadur Singh with Arti and Rajesh, 1996*

*The Varmas with Bahadur Singh's family, 1996*

*Breaking bread: Bahadur Singh hosts a warm welcome, 2008*

*The second generation—Rajesh and Karnail, December 2008*

*Bahadur Singh with Abhinav, December 2008*

*A bond preserved by generations, 2008*

*A descendent of Mini the cow, 2008*

*The fourth generation in action under Jarnail's watchful eye*

1

2

*Gur making: A family tradition*

3

4

*Sweet memories*

*Former Prime Minister Dr Manmohan Singh releasing a commemorative stamp in honour of Prabodh Chandra, 2005, New Delhi*

# The Reunion

AFTER I got married in 1994, my wife Arti and I visited India in 1996. During our visit to the North, we went to Amritsar. The only night we stayed there, we spent at my friend Gunbir's house. I had known Gunbir since my student days in Chandigarh in 1981–82. Like many families, Gunbir's was a joint family too and his family lived with his parents under one roof.

After spending a night with them, the next morning my friend Gunbir's father Mr Dalbir Singh arranged for us to visit the Golden Temple, one of the holiest places of worship for Sikhs. Mr Dalbir Singh was not only a learned man, but also a successful industrialist, who was well connected. He knew a senior member of the management committee of the temple who arranged for us a special viewing of the relics of Sikh warriors—a symbol of sacrifice for the sake of a cause.

Arti and I were shown the bows and arrows, the shields, the armour and swords used by warriors of the past. The sword, an inspiring symbol that Shingara Singh always carried with him; a symbol that became the cause for him to be sentenced to death; the death sentence, the result of a loyalty that became the foundation of a bond between Bahadur Singh, my father, and Uncle Prabodh. And that bond was passed on to me, in the form of a story, and now it was a permanent memory; the memory of my childhood days spent at Ghasitpura, with Bahadur Singh's family in the village. Yes, Ghasitpura the village on road that connected Amritsar with Batala, my hometown. And we were going to pass through Ghasitpura on our way to Quadian, a small town eight miles east of Batala.

We left Amritsar around 1.00 p.m. The taxi driver was ferrying three of us—me, my wife Arti, and one of my friends Bhupinder who had joined us for the road trip.

I had made up my mind to look for the Bahadur Singh family. I was sitting in the front passenger seat of the taxi, to make sure that I had a clear view of where we were going and I could give instructions to the driver in case I recognized any landmark.

Forget villages, even towns did not have any road signs indicating where we were. No wonder I was having a hard

THE REUNION

time locating the village. I knew it was about five miles south of Batala, the town we had moved to from New Delhi at the request of my uncle. We stopped the taxi at a few places asking people about Ghasitpura, and finally got near the village. I remembered that Bahadur Singh's dwelling was to the west of the road.

Finally, I stopped a young boy on a bicycle, and asked him for Jarnail Singh's or Bahadur Singh's house; not sure if Bahadur Singh was still alive. The boy knew the family. He said, 'Hop on to the back of my bicycle I will take you to Bahadur Singh.' I did and the taxi followed.

My father had undertaken the same journey from Batala to Ghasitpura thirty-four years ago. The only difference was that he went five miles to the south of Batala, while I was headed towards Batala, now five miles away to the north.

The moment of truth came. I saw Bahadur Singh, touched his feet and could not hold back my tears. I broke down. He was still the same, nothing had changed. Bahadur Singh held me tight in his arms, and said, 'Since your father left town, it's as if I lost both my arms. Your father, my Bauji, was the support I needed when I am this old. I have no one left. But, I still have enough strength in these arms to hold my Bauji's son. You cared to think of visiting me. Now I am very happy.'

We sat down on a cot. Thirty-four years ago, my father Bhushan had sat with Bahadur Singh on a similar cot. I introduced Arti to him as his newest daughter-in-law and she touched his feet and sought his blessings. Thirty-four years ago, Bahadur Singh's wife, Bibi, who was Shingara Singh's widow, had touched my father's feet, seeking his blessings. And here was Arti, my wife, thirty-four years later, not too far from the exact same spot, where the exact same thing occurred between my father and Bahadur Singh's deceased wife who had been Shingara Singh's widow and whom we all affectionately called Bibi.

Bahadur Singh asked if he could have a word with me and requested me to follow him to a corner, behind a mud wall. I was perplexed. He asked me if he could borrow some money. I had few hundred-rupee notes in the left pocket of my pants. I did not count them and gave him the whole bunch. He kept only five notes and gave back the rest. He cried and said that ours was a totally unexpected and a surprise arrival. He felt very small and ashamed that he did not have anything to give to his youngest daughter-in-law, my wife Arti, who was visiting him for the first time. Bibi, Bahadur Singh's wife would have normally taken care of important occasions such as this one, but she was no more. He did not have cash in the house. He promised me that the next time we visited him, this would not happen. We hugged each other and finally, holding each other, we both cried.

We sat together for about an hour, talking about days gone by. Bahadur Singh reminded me of my boyhood days—days when he would come early in the morning to milk our cows. One of those cows was a deep rusty-brown colour and we named her Mini. On many occasions when Bahadur Singh was milking Mini, I would run down, with a 10-ounce stainless steel tumbler in my hand. I would watch Mini licking and grooming her young calf, while Bahadur Singh would be milking Mini. And he would squirt fresh milk and fill my tumbler, which I would finish in a few gulps. I thought of the days when, even in my innocence, I knew the true source of milk.

As my own memories carried me away into my past, Bahadur Singh's gentle whisper brought me back to where I was, in the present, in his company. 'Do you remember that rusty-brown Mini? That was the cow that I had insisted your father should buy when he and I became friends. A cow is a symbol of prosperity. Your father listened to me. And that is how you ended up drinking fresh milk from that cow. Look at you. Cow's milk is the reason you are a healthy, intelligent and strong young man. And you will be happy to know that I have kept the lineage of Mini alive—I have one cow and two oxen from her lineage. They, and the frozen memories of the past, are the only living reminders of my association with your father and your family. You all are gone,' he said sadly, 'I do not even have a picture of you, or my Bauji, or your brother, or sister. I have nothing left from those wonderful days, except for them.' He pointed to one cow and two oxen walking back from their daily grazing and work routine. The cow was rusty-brown colour, an exact replica of Mini, as I remembered her.

I ran towards her and touched her forehead. She was calm and seemed to be at peace. She let me touch her, pat her on her forehead and gazed at me, as though trying to recognize me. Bahadur Singh, having caught up with us, said, 'Look at the cow, she leaves in the morning and having wandered about the whole day comes back to her spot, her anchor, back to where her calf is, back to where her home is, back to where she belongs—just like us humans. We also keep coming back to where we think we belong. I am so happy that you also have come back, though for a short visit. This cow,' he continued, 'is a reminder of my family's relationship with your father that goes back to the times of the war[3], even before India was independent. I have always reminded Jarnail and Karnail that after I am gone, they have to make sure that they keep the lineage from Mini going. This livestock is a constant reminder to all of us of the sacred bond that has existed between the two families, a bond that was formed when destiny brought my elder brother and your father together.'

He turned to look at me, 'I hope maybe one day, when you and Arti have children, you will come back, if not for good, at least for a short visit. I will not be here, but everything else

---

[3] World War II

will still be here; my great-grandchildren and the offspring from these animals, this dwelling and this village, everything. I hope you and your wife will keep coming back. This will enable you to build new memories and hopefully help connect your children to their roots.'

Listening to Bahadur Singh, summarizing the meaning of life so succinctly was very powerful—memories of a bond and its symbolic representation as a young cow and a calf; the temporary nature of human life; our desire to hold on to something tangible; our desire to pass on our memories.

I imagined Bahadur Singh sharing stories with Jaila, similar to those my father had shared with me when I was a young boy. And maybe even this one with a hope that Jaila would pass it on to his children and grandchildren. 'You are a very wise man,' I said to him. 'You have taught me something that they did not teach me in colleges and universities I attended. You have enlightened me with the essence of life that I can live and experience, and perhaps pass on to my children. The truth is, with all the life experiences you have, you are a very wise and rich man. These wrinkles on your forehead are the signs of your age and your wisdom. The unconditional love and acceptance you have shown towards me and Arti has filled our lives with a treasure more precious than anything all the money in the world could buy. And the memory of this love and acceptance is going to stay with me and Arti forever.'

Bahadur Singh simply looked at me and gave me an innocent smile, and said, 'You are so educated, settled in a distant and a prosperous land, you have seen the whole world. On the other hand, my life has simply revolved around this village, or around your family and your house in Batala. It feels as though it was only yesterday when Bauji was here, you were all together as a family, and your father's elder brother was around. Whenever your Uncle Prabodh visited Batala, he would make it a point to look for me. I remember, once he even asked me to ride with him in his official car. I accompanied him and he visited my family in the village, spending an hour with me and my family. That is the extent of my experiences in life.'

As Bahadur Singh mentioned my father and Uncle Prabodh, I was suddenly reminded of the beginning of it all. How it all started and I wanted to know about the missing piece.

I asked Bahadur Singh if he knew any details about his elder brother Shingara Singh assaulting a British Army officer who had dishonoured my father—Bahadur Singh's Bauji and Shingara Singh's Sahib.

Bahadur Singh looked deeply into my eyes and said in his tender voice, 'I knew one day you would ask me this question. Bauji also knew, perhaps, that this question might be asked of me one more time and perhaps that is the reason your father wanted me to save telling you about it until the time was right. I think the day has come.'

Bahadur Singh got up from the cot and asked me to come inside the room, the room made from mud walls and bricks.

He slowly bent down and pulled out an old suitcase from beneath a cot covered with a worn-out bedsheet and blankets. The suitcase was not locked and Bahadur Singh dug into the rear right corner of the suitcase, underneath some other valuables that must have meant something of importance to him. Gently he pulled out an envelope and handed it over to me.

I knew right away what it was. It was the same envelope that Bahadur Singh had given to my father Bhushan. It was the same envelope that had a letter from Shingara Singh, the same letter that Shingara Singh had narrated to Bapu, the village elder, who had first introduced my father to Bahadur Singh back in 1963–64. It was the same letter that my father could not read because he did not know how to read Punjabi. I was lucky. I knew how to read and write Punjabi, a language I became proficient in because our family moved to Batala in the state of Punjab, when I was a little boy.

I could not wait to read the letter. I asked Bahadur Singh if I could open the envelope, without realizing that it was not sealed anymore. The faded and partially smeared name of Shingara Singh was still visible. Although time had done all it could to make Shingara Singh disappear in the past, but that was not meant to be. The bonds of destiny were far stronger and had outlived time. Shingara Singh's story had survived. I knew that he had passed on his story successfully.

Bahadur Singh told me that the envelope was now mine to keep. I put that envelope into the duffle bag I was carrying. I would read it later, I decided. Bahadur Singh asked me to sit with him outside in the sun. It was obvious to me that he wanted to spend as much time as he could just sitting with me and reminiscing about our shared past, when I was a little boy and Bahadur Singh was my father's special employee in the factory. We talked about the days when Uncle Prabodh would visit with us and during every one of those visits he would make it a point to spend few minutes with Bahadur Singh, as if simply to remind him that regardless of his position, Uncle Prabodh still remembered and valued Shingara Singh's deep association with Bhushan, his younger brother, my father's love and respect for Shingara Singh, and Shingara Singh's loyalty towards Bhushan.

Bahadur Singh knew that I was not the same little boy, who would do anything to be with him, while visiting Ghasitpura. He knew that now I had become a man, a man who could afford many things in life, but could not afford free time; a man who was there, visiting Ghasitpura, trying to look at the canvas of his past. To admire that huge canvas just one more time, a canvas on which Bahadur Singh was a mere little dot.

As we were sitting, talking and reminiscing our past,

Bahadur Singh's daughter and her husband drove in. Her husband was driving the family-owned scooter, with Bahadur Singh's daughter perched on the back seat.

Back in 1974–75 the same daughter, Harjeet, used to study at Baring College, the college I had graduated from. At that time I had changed my major from Pre-Medicine to Economics and Literature, while she had just started her Pre-Med programme. She failed to make it to medical school, but did get into nursing school.

Now Harjeet was a nurse working in a government-run Primary Health Care Centre in a village near Quadian, a small town about eight miles from Batala. Her husband was a school teacher in a village near where they lived. I told her that we were on our way to Quadian, where we planned to spend the night visiting one of our friends, Lakhwinder. She insisted that we visit her the following morning. She gave me an additional incentive of a makki ki roti and saag meal, an incentive that I did not really need. The next morning, Arti, Bhupinder, Lakhi and I visited Harjeet in her modest village home and spent few hours with her husband and her son.

It felt good visiting with her and seeing she lived a decent life and was married to a loving and caring husband. My father's insisting to Bahadur Singh that Harjeet must go to college seemed to have paid off.

# A Bet We Both Won

During our visit with Bahadur Singh in December 1996, he had promised my wife Arti and me that he was not going to die until he saw our children. My bet against myself was that I would visit India only if Bahadur Singh was alive and was able to bless my children.

Thereafter, when we returned to the US, Arti and I decided to enter a new phase of our married life—we decided to start a family. In December of 1997 we were blessed with our first child, a son. We named him Abhinav after my dear friend Abhinav Upadhyay.

The silent bet I had made with myself was always at the back of my mind. I was acutely aware of Bahadur Singh's advanced age. This awareness, combined with the knowledge of how my father Bhushan had lost all those precious years before he reconnected with Shingara Singh's family, meant I could not wait for the day when we would meet Bahadur Singh again. Days turned into weeks, and then quickly turned into months and years. In April 2000, we were blessed with our second child, our daughter Meera, a name taken after a medieval Indian saint-poet who was a devotee of Lord Krishna.

Raising two children without much of a support system made the time go by fast. Before we knew it was 2008. Abhinav was ten, and Meera eight-plus years old. We decided that this would be a good time to visit India and pass on my bond with the Ghasitpura family to Abhinav and Meera. For us as a family, this visit to India also meant visiting Bahadur Singh and his family in the village and seeking his blessings for our family of four.

We set aside one day for visiting Bahadur Singh and his family in Ghasitpura. I got in touch with two of my childhood friends whom I had known since 1964—Harbhajan and Ramesh, both physicians and settled in Batala. Harbhajan was Batala's Chief Medical Officer and Ramesh had a private practice that included a small hospital. At the back of my mind, I felt it would also be good for Bahadur Singh and his family to know physicians in the closest town, Batala. Both my friends graciously agreed to take time to come to Ghasitpura and spend the day with us.

Our children Abhinav and Meera did not know what to expect during the visit. There was no way Arti and I could think of preparing them for their experience in a village—the village I used to frequent forty years ago, the village where Shingara Singh had once lived. Shingara Singh, an ordinary man with extraordinary courage, a man who was not afraid of sacrificing his life to protect my father's honour. How could I explain to a ten-year old and an eight-year old that in the village lived a family not related to us by blood, but that their relationship with me and before me, with my father and my uncle, had been born out of destiny; that it had been preserved out of choice—a choice my father made back in 1960s when he reconnected with Shingara Singh's family members and his younger brother Bahadur Singh. And that three decades later in 1996, their mother and I had made a conscious choice to reconnect with Bahadur Singh and his family and that now in 2008 we were going to meet them again.

From Amritsar, the city of Golden Temple, we made our way to Ghasitpura. To cover a distance of 40 kilometres, it took us about an hour-and-a-half. We arrived at Ghasitpura around 1.30 p.m. This time, compared to my previous visit of 1996, finding the village was much easier.

Bahadur Singh had been waiting for us since noon on a lean patch of the dirt road that connected the family house to the main road. Since our last visit in 1994, the dirt road had been upgraded, now it was partially laid with bricks.

As soon as I got off the rented van, and I was the first one to do so, I bowed down almost touching Bahadur Singh's feet, and sought his blessings. Right away, I reminded him of the bet we had made during our prior visit—that he was going to live long enough to bless my children. I also reminded Bahadur Singh of the promise we had made during my previous visit that Arti and I would show him 'some tangible results' and would start working on having a family. The sparkle in Bahadur Singh's eyes, and his beaming smile conveyed more than any words could. Bahadur Singh asked me to translate for Abhinav and Meera that he had been waiting for this day since Arti and I had visited him last, back in December 1996 before either of them was born.

Bahadur Singh and I hugged each other. He wanted to simply hold me, perhaps to make up for the twelve years since we had met last. That warm expression of welcome and affection did not leave anything that needed saying at that moment. Language had failed. Then I handed Bahadur Singh his walking cane. He held it in his right hand, while I held his left hand. We started walking together towards the family home. Even at ninety-three, Bahadur Singh was alert and his steps confident. He walked without making any halts, although slowly. He very clearly remembered our last visit.

The family members waiting for us included Bahadur Singh's three sons, and their respective families that included their children and grandchildren. The family had prepared for us makki ki roti and saag, topped with fresh home-made butter, lentils, rice, vegetables and fresh milk. For dessert, we were served freshly made brown-sugar pellets topped with fresh peanuts.

After lunch, Jarnail Singh, known to me as Jaila while growing up, wanted Abhinav and Meera to see the making of fresh jaggery (raw brown-sugar pellets made from fresh sugarcane). The site was not too far. The process was in full swing and the mild fermented smell of the boiling sugarcane juice permeated the small room where a huge six-feet wide wok was being used to boil the sugarcane juice and evaporate all the water. A giant fire pit in the ground was fuelled by the dried-up pulp of sugarcane from which the juice had already been squeezed out maybe the night before.

The ambience brought frozen memories from the distant past back to life, when as a young eight-year old I would visit the village with my parents, elder brother and younger sister. This was the best part of the whole experience—huddled in that small room awed by that huge twenty-five-gallon wok, simmering with viscous hot brown-sugar; a huge wooden spatula that we would use to very gently stir the contents in the wok. The temperature had to be just right. Otherwise, the whole lot would have a burnt odour to it. And maintaining the right temperature meant someone had to control how much air and fuel to feed. Nothing was wasted. The ash would be mixed with soil in the fields.

Here in the present, gentle strokes of that huge wooden spatula scratching against the bottom of the wok, and gently bursting bubbles of that simmering hot, highly viscous brown-sugar sounded as if it was raining and someone was rowing a boat—trying to go back in time.

While Abhinav, Meera and Arti watched this fascinating operation, Jaila reminisced about our times in the late 1960s when I would visit Ghasitpura, spend the whole day with my family, enjoying myself watching the very same activities that Abhinav and Meera were enjoying almost fifty years later, joy that comes from enjoying simple things. Standing next to me, Jaila movingly recalled, 'I watched you growing up. I remember you and your family's visits with us during the winter months. I remember that you used to be a part of this whole routine. It was so much fun for all of us. Since then, I have watched my own children and later their children enjoying the very same things that you enjoyed, experiencing those moments of a simple village life. The only difference is that for us it is a way of life, while for you it is a way of keeping your placental cord with your past alive, and passing it on to your children. It would have been wonderful if you all could have stayed with us for a few days. Your children would have had an opportunity to play with my grandchildren. Nevertheless, we all, especially my father, are so fortunate that you have taken the time to bring your family to visit us in this humble house. We may not have been able to offer you anything that you are used to in your life in America, but we offered you our heart. Also, for your children, we wanted to make sure that they get to see all you used to enjoy during your visits with us—when you were the age Abhinav and Meera are now. That is why we started the whole operation of making jaggery early this morning. When you used to visit us as a child, you would have the whole day to spend with us and enjoy yourself; I knew your children would have only few hours. Now I am watching your children, who until this day, had no connection with these fields, with this dirt, with these animals. I am hoping that after this visit, they will carry fond memories of the short time with us. I am hoping that this visit will provide you and your children enough reasons to visit back to this village not too far in the future.'

Bahadur Singh's grandchildren showed Abhinav and Meera around the wide spectrum of activities young children get involved in with suspended disbelief, and here that meant activities primarily revolving around what is happening out in the field and the daily routine that comes with taking care of livestock.

It was around 2.30 p.m. when Abhinav and Meera were done with their round of the surroundings, and Arti and I decided to spend some time with Bahadur Singh, sitting on the cot next to him. He reminded us of our last visit with him and he specifically mentioned that since our visit last time was unannounced, he had not been able to prepare a welcome. This time he was more than prepared. From the right pocket of his long kurta, he took out a gold ring and asked us if it was okay with us if he gave that ring to Abhinav, our son. Both, Arti and I were not only very moved, but also, in a way amused and delighted that despite his advanced age, Bahadur Singh remembered every detail from our last visit from ten years ago—including the fact that he felt uncomfortable, since he could not give a gift to Arti when he saw her the first time.

We asked Abhinav to touch Bahadur Singh's feet and seek his blessings. Bahadur Singh did not expect an American born boy to follow the old Indian tradition. He told me he was proud that I married Arti, who he thought was doing a great job in passing traditions on to the next generation.

After my son Abhinav got the ring, he took me aside and whispered, 'Papa I do not fully understand the meaning of all this, but I feel it is very important and it makes me feel connected.' Listening to a ten-year old describe his feelings so succinctly, made me feel proud and I felt that the real purpose of bringing my children to be blessed by Bahadur Singh had been accomplished. The bond of destiny had been ceremoniously passed over to the next generation, just as my father had passed it on to me. There was a difference, nevertheless. In my case it was through a passive act of listening, in the case of Abhinav and Meera it was accomplished by their active participation in the story. My hope is that this bond of destiny will be protected, preserved, nurtured and hopefully passed on so that the story continues.

# The Letter

*Respected Sahib*

*Do you remember that just like you I also wanted to learn how to write? I also wanted to tell my story. Sahib, I could not get enough time in this life to learn how to write all this. But I did learn how to write my name in English.*

*My life seems to be cheating me, as I do not have much time left. I know that you will come looking for me one day, but by that time it may be too late. And I do not want to die without telling you what happened that night, the night when we all had a lot of fun; the night when everything changed for you and for me.*

*Sahib, after the dinner was over and things had died*

*down I was still thinking about what had happened that afternoon. I did not like it that the man violated not only the army code of conduct but also my Sahib's honour, while I did nothing. Not because I was afraid Sahib, but because I did not want to correct one wrong by committing another.*

*That night I was getting angry, so I decided to take a walk along the banks of the river. If you remember Sahib, it was a moonless night, and overcast. It was while I was walking on the banks that I came across him.*

*I stopped and asked if I could have a word with him. Then I told him that what he did that afternoon was not how we, as soldiers, had been taught to behave. He should not have done what he did. Then I also told him that if such a thing were to happen again I would do everything to protect my Sahib and his honour. As my Sahib's ardali, it was my duty and I would not fail in my duty, regardless of the consequences.*

*No sooner than I was finished talking Sahib, he again started cursing you and not only that, he surprised me by assaulting me. He knocked me down and began punching me with one hand and choking me with the other. He almost suffocated me to death Sahib, he was trying to kill me.*

*Thankfully, I was carrying my small knife and my holy book with me. I was able to get the strength to reach my knife and use it to protect myself. In the struggle that ensued, I accidentally ended up killing him, not because I wanted to Sahib. I was merely trying to defend myself. I was so afraid of what had just happened, that I dumped his body in that monsoon-swollen river.*

*I am very sorry for all the trouble I caused you Sahib.*

*I wish there was a way that I could ask for your forgiveness in person. Unfortunately, I do not think that is going to happen.*

*I hope Sahib, as always, you will have a big heart to forgive your ardali.*

*May God always be with you, to protect you and your honour.*

*I remain, your ardali,*

*Shingara Singh*

(Translated by the author from the original Gurumukhi)

# Epilogue

## Lady Reid

Lady Reid was the wife of His Excellency Sir Robert Neil Reid, the Governor of Indian State of Assam (1937–1942) and the High Commissioner of British India. An active philanthropist, Lady Reid actively worked with the tribes of North-East India. Reid Chest Hospital in Jhalupara, Shillong, (then in the state of Assam) still stands as a silent testimony to her commitment to the tribal people of the area.

She laid the foundation stone of this hospital on 15 November 1939, and the hospital was inaugurated on 20 January 1943 by Lady Linlithgow, wife of British Governor General and Viceroy of India, Lord Linlithgow (1936–1943).

The initiative to set up this hospital had been taken by the Tuberculosis Association of Assam, with the backing of the King-Emperor's Tuberculosis Fund and the King George's Thanksgiving Fund.

Ironically, Shingara Singh died of tuberculosis sometime in 1948 because of lack of treatment.

### Bahadur Singh

Bahadur Singh passed away peacefully in December 2015, at the age of 99.

### Dr Ashwani Kumar

Dr Ashwani Kumar was a Member of the Upper House of the Indian Parliament, the Rajya Sabha, and was also a member of the Council of Ministers under the leadership of Prime Minister Dr Manmohan Singh. Dr Kumar, who is a Senior Advocate of Supreme Court of India, was married to Madhu, who passed away in November 2012. Their son Ashish is married to Vanya, and the family lives in New Delhi.

Dr Kumar's daughter Urvashi lives with her son and husband in Dubai.

### Rajesh and Arti Varma

Married since 1994, Rajesh and Arti live with their two wonderful angels Abhinav and Meera in Burbank, California.

EPILOGUE

## Bhushan a.k.a Dev Brat Varma

Bhushan lived in Batala from 1963 to 1987, when he migrated to the United States to join his two sons Rakesh and Rajesh. He passed away in 2002. His daughter Richa lives with her family in England.

## Prabodh Chandra

Prabodh Chandra passed away in 1986 at the age of 75.

# Acknowledgements

During my twenty-five-year long journey to complete this chronicle I have received much help from my friends, co-workers, mentors and many others who have kindly provided me valuable suggestions and encouragement to keep moving forward. I would like to acknowledge all of these important companions. I hope that the final result does not disappoint them. Whether or not it does, I would like to state that their help I will always remember.

I owe my deep gratitude to respected Gulzar Sahib, my mentor on this project.

For initial edits, I would like to thank Late Dr Paul L. Love of American College, Madurai; Bhupinder Parihar Aziz for his transcreations; Edgar Garcia from Yale and Mona Khanna of Chicago for their initial reads and feedback.

My sincere thanks are due to Rakesh, my brother for reminding me many of details about our father Bhushan, which had receded into my memory, and to Bunny bhaiya for telling me many things about Bhushan that I did not know.

I owe my thanks also to Alexandra and Mark Helfrich of Burbank, and to Abhinav Upadhyay who was the first person to read the draft at the stage when it was a personal narrative, and who encouraged me to keep at it and turn it into a book.

I want to thank Ammu bhaiya and Madhu bhabhi for sharing their family treasures.

I want to express my thanks to Kapish ji at Rupa Publishers for bringing this project to you because he believed that the story would touch some corner of your heart. I would also like to thank the Rupa team for taking my long phone calls as they worked with me for the final edits and for the cover artwork that captures the essence of the book.

To my wife Arti I would want to say, without your patient sacrifice of those long evenings when you would wait for me to finish writing and finally give up on the sofa, every evening, for all those long years—this book would not have been possible. And had you not taken those compelling pictures, this would have been a silent story. And to my dearest children Abhi and Meera I want to thank you for allowing me to take away our family time.

Thanks to my parents-in-law for sharing their stories with my children so that one day they can pass them on to their children.

And finally, my thanks to all the individuals whose story it is.